3 Nights of the Perseids

3 NIGHTS OF THE PERSEIDS

Poems by

Ned Balbo

The University of Evansville Press
Evansville, Indiana

The text of this book is composed in Baskerville.
Composition by R.G.
Manufacturing by Thomson-Shore.
Book and Cover Design: W.B. & R.G.

Library of Congress Cataloging-in-Publication Data

Names: Balbo, Ned, 1959- author.
Title: 3 nights of the Perseids.
Other titles: Three nights of the Perseids
Description: First edition. | Evansville, IN : The University of Evansville
    Press, [2018] | Includes bibliographical references.
Identifiers: LCCN 2018048210| ISBN 9780930982782 (hardcover) | ISBN
    0930982789 (hardcover)
Subjects: LCSH: American poetry.
Classification: LCC PS3552.A4454 A6 2018 | DDC 811/.54--dc23
LC record available at https://lccn.loc.gov/2018048210

2 Bridges Review, *Alabama Literary Review*, *Angle*, *Birmingham Poetry Review*, *Cimarron
Review*, *The Dark Horse*, *Delaware Poetry Review*, *Dogwood*, *Ecotone*, *First Things*, Indolent
Books/*"What Rough Beast," Italian Americana*, *Light*, *Measure*, *The New Criterion*, *The
New Verse News*, *North Dakota Quarterly*, *Poets Reading the News*, *Potomac Review*, *Rattle*,
Rondeau Roundup, *Scoundrel Time*, *String Poet*, *Studio*, and *Think Journal*.

"London Crowds and Tory Crimes" first appeared in the *Clash by Night: an anthology
inspired by the Clash's* London Calling (CityLit Press), edited by Gerry LaFemina and
Gregg Wilhelm.

Epigraph sources:
Maggie Gray, "Perseids," *The Junket*, January 14, 2015.
David Bowie, "Five Years," *The Rise and Fall of Ziggy Stardust and the Spiders from
    Mars*, RCA, 1972.
Lucretius, *The Nature of Things* (A. E. Stallings, translator), Penguin, 2007.
Albert Goldbarth, "The Future," *Great Topics of the World*, Picador, 1995.
Martial, *Selected Epigrams* (Susan McLean, translator), University of Wisconsin
    Press, 2014.

The University of Evansville Press
1800 Lincoln Avenue
Evansville, IN 47722
(812) 488-2963

I'd like to extend thanks to the Vermont Studio Center, the Virginia Center for the Creative Arts, Poetry by the Sea, the West Chester University Poetry Conference, and the Writing the Rockies Annual Conference for welcome support.

A special thanks to friends, colleagues, and students in the MFA program in Creative Writing and Environment at Iowa State University and the English Department at Loyola University Maryland.

Among those extending invaluable encouragement are Kim Bridgford, Erica Dawson, Rhina Espaillat, Dana Gioia, Rob Griffith, Sam Gwynn, Mike Juster, Katie Darby Mullins, Angela Alaimo O'Donnell, Ron Patkus, David Rothman, Beth Spires, David St. John, Maria Terrone, Dan Tobin, Lesley Wheeler, and David Yezzi. Much gratitude, also, to Tony Barnstone, Stephen Kampa, and Timothy Steele. Andrew Hudgins, Mark Jarman, Charles Martin: thanks for the inspiration.

For support and kindness above and beyond: thank you, Debra Marquart.

With meteors above and wren in hand: love and thanks to Jane.

CONTENTS

III.

IV.

Rare Book and Reader

Helen D. Lockwood Library, September 1977

Back in the days when we called freshmen *freshmen*,
I was one, a lank-haired Vassar co-ed
newly landed, searching for the reason
I was there. Before me, dead ahead,
the future held its promise like the shaded
vistas in brochures, or like an album
on the rack the moment you've decided
that you have to buy it, take it home —

And so I felt (caught in that no man's land
of post-arrival limbo, nothing sure
except how much I didn't understand
of privilege, wealth, and class), this much was clear:
the album's title — *Past, Present, and Future* —
and the cloak of Marvel's Doctor Strange
vanishing through some portal on the cover
promised an escape — at least a change.

The last track was inspired by Nostradamus
Gallic seer and astrologer
who wrote *The Prophecies,* mysterious
quatrains of cryptic riddles that declare
foreknowledge of disaster, plague, and war,
offering hints that tease and tantalize
(through allegory, tangled metaphor)
the gullible who read with opened eyes —

Hister (Hitler?), *three brothers* (Kennedys?)
world wars (all three?) — well, sure, he could be wrong,
but if Al Stewart thought the prophecies
troubling enough to put them in a song,
what else would time confirm before too long?
I sat, the huge book open to a page
five hundred years old, in a foreign tongue
(French mostly), brought out carefully from storage

by a young librarian, or senior,
watchful and amused at my expense.
Who wouldn't be? She knew I was no scholar
steeped in sixteenth-century charlatans,
but just some boy who'd wandered in by chance
or impulse, new to college, drifting still,
his mind enraptured by coincidence
proclaimed as proof, each generation's will

to buy such bunk, as always, bottomless.
Now I'd beheld an ur-text, reassured
it did exist. A reader under glass,
I sat, sealed in the hush, but not one word —
archaic, clue-encoded — struck a chord:
I'd never studied French! And yet I'd seen
the priceless artifact kept under guard
in some dark vault climate-controlled within

the labyrinthine archives I envisioned;
briefly exposed to light and then returned
to deep oblivion, the world's end
unknown and waiting. What else had I learned?

That where the distant future is concerned,
no language equal to it can exist
nor is there language clear and unadorned
to show how time recedes into the past

— Or if there is, it's written not for us
but for the eyes of one whose practiced gaze
sees farther than our own — who knows that loss
becomes the weight and measure of our days —
who, in the hidden turnings of a phrase,
detects a revelation cast in code
we almost grasp but which remains, always,
unbroken, like the mercy that we're owed.

I.

The brightest are written into works of art as omens, harbingers of political turmoil and manmade calamity — but they are also reminders of the celestial menace behind the Perseids' pretty displays. Meteoroid, meteor, meteorite; we give the rocks new titles as they complete their searing rite of passage down to earth, and for centuries we've scanned the skies for anything that would really conquer us in the event of a collision.

— Maggie Gray, "Perseids"

The Underground Tour

Into the street beneath the street we step,
denizens of Seattle Underground
for now, as purplish light through sidewalk glass
streaks down upon the tour group that we've joined
for kicks, for entertainment, for an hour.
Our guide — voluble, rotund — tells of fire,
a tinderbox laid waste, and city fathers,
patrons of banks and brothels, who rebuilt
the whole place one flight up, the world they knew
submerged in shadow, ill-lit corridors
infested with rats and vice, brief assignations
between supply and human frailty,
neither at risk of ever running out.
You don't look like you're having too much fun,
though I enjoy this sort of thing: the sweep
of great deeds and decay, the roar of time
down history's tunnel past the glass and brickwork,
leaving us, and rubble, in its wake.
Toy settlers trapped in dusty dioramas —
check. A few framed photos of the past
from some high point: a teeming Wild West town,
it seems, fists and saloon doors swinging freely
— *Forward*, our tour guide beckons, into chambers
more like catacombs, the street-glow gone,
replaced by blinding bulbs. I touch your hand.
More tales of opium dens — speakeasies, too —
tactfully sanitized for daytime tours.
Rough concrete yields to nailed plywood planks

and more smashed remnants: shattered wooden pipe,
a teller's cage, wrecked gears the size of bike wheels,
even a round once-scarlet sofa ditched,
bedecked in dust. ("They used it on the set
of some old TV movie filmed down here.")
Up there's where we'll go next, you want to say,
and soon, you hope: you've had your fill of news
a century old, facades of storefronts closed
like history itself, a box shut tight
despite the clues it scatters in plain sight.
I'm having fun — an hour's worth of legend,
facts and guesses mixed to give us myths,
our earthly comedy — but, all alone,
I'd never go. The only point's to share
it with someone — with you — who passes by
me with the crowd, nervous before the entry
to another junk-strewn, mildewed grotto
that may hold the key to some lost past,
or only dirt, old plumbing. Left alone,
what would this place be like if some swift blackout
cut the lights? Don't ask. We're not alone —
you're with me, I'm with you, Pioneer Square
unseen above, the Tlingit Totem Pole
that arson torched re-carved with tribal blessings
and resentments tall against gray sky
toward which we'll climb, in time . . . . Finally, the steep
drop of the catwalk's last stretch, more loose boards —
I gently touch your sleeve to hold you back,
and step ahead, decisive, vigilant
that you emerge unhurt, safe from the fears
that made you hesitate, give in once more,
and forge on by my side . . . . "Let me go first,"
I say, and mean it, as you watch me pass.

A Nylon Cape, a Fall of Snow

My hair falls, grayer still with every haircut,
sliding white or silver down the cape,
soon to be brushed away or shaken out
when I stand up. The clipper's glide-and-scrape
has run its course and shaved me to the skin,
except on top. The barber, snipping still,
talks gently, wears the same scalp he was born in,
wielding scissors with unflinching skill.
How strange to watch time fall away discarded
to the checkered tile, the chair's chrome base . . .
What fads or fashions thrived, died out, departed
sadly, while blades clicked away? A trace
of Barbicide, more vital than Vitalis,
stings the air . . . . He's done. *I doubt he'll tell us.*

Time's Passage at Whiskey River

"Free Beer Tomorrow"

I read the sign. It's late. Tomorrow's near —
The beer's flat. No one taps another keg.
The shortstop stumbles on the runner's leg,
while frozen strangers balance at the bar,
slow-motion gestures wasted on the air.
Outside, the tattooed girl takes one more drag
while friendly foes attack the punching bag
that offers glory to the challenger
with change to spare. Surprised, the shortstop blinks,
eyes flashing back and forth in diamond dust —
Young men with sunken cheeks wait for the drinks
the tattooed girl withholds, because she must,
when all our hopes, past midnight, turn to sorrow —
There's no free beer today, and none tomorrow.

3 Nights of the Perseids

The night sky's space-debris is radiant
if you can see it, every meteor
a casualty or lost cause in this shower
unsurpassed for 3 nights every August
from my balcony: the Perseids.
A comet's castoffs breach the atmosphere,

more shooting stars that graze the stratosphere.
My spotting scope's fixed to a gradient
the better to receive the Perseids
before they vanish, each small light a tear
we might take as a sign or augury
of what's to come, or not: before a shower

of fortune rains or lessens, when its hour
arrives at its own pace. Though not one sphere —
fiery, imperfect — blows past in a gust
of solar wind, small bodies radiate
from somewhere: flying beetles, meteors
of chitin that collide like Perseus,

Andromeda, and fate, pursuing us.
I glimpse a rapid, brief celestial show
in my peripheral vision, meteors
my scope obscured but you saw, sharp and clear,
a stubborn gaze the best ingredient
for awe rewarded, suddenly, in August,

here in Iowa, where you're a guest —
bound for the East Coast when the Perseids
are over, saddened by the radius
our jobs impose, no quick fix in our power . . .
We live with it. Across the hemisphere,
a waning crescent pales, no meteorites

reported; here, a clockwork cosmos meets
horizons that a greater dark augments.
A jet's lights flash, too far away to fear,
and we can tell its contrails from persistent
trains, gases dissolving in a shower
of ionized traces, white streaks radiant —

How far away they fly: what skies they pierce,
whose lives they meet or tear with every shower
on their august return, still radiant.

High Strangeness

The degree of "strangeness" is certainly one aspect of
a filtered UFO report. The higher the "strangeness index" the
more the information aspects of the report defy explanation . . . ;
in short, did the strange thing really happen?
— J. Allen Hynek

The "Saturn disc" reported
back in '54,
ringed sphere against the sky
was not the first recorded
nor do we know why
it hovered for an hour

then vanished like a ghost
into upwelling dust.
It was, we knew at once,
extraterrestrial.
Before and ever since,
far-flung, celestial

unearthly craft in shapes
compressed or spherical
surveil us by night —
Triangular "tear-drops"
that shed a greenish light
eyewitnesses recall,

still shocked by their encounters
through space or time, or both,
tracked down against their will.

Your job's to calm their fears
and coax out every detail.
Place no one under oath —

They may be sensitive —
persons whose faith is challenged
by the very concept —
their world upended, changed
by truths they can't accept
or, with a wave, disprove.

When they describe abduction
from farms in Minnesota,
crop circles and burnt embers,
their missing son or daughter
lured in some seduction
no one quite remembers

unprodded, nod your head,
and take notes, copious notes —
They may recount instead
the raising of a wand
that scattered sheep and goats,
the silvery gloved hand

whose touch could paralyze
a witness or stop time.
Charred metal, shards of glass
are clues to analyze
if we can gather some
before they're lost; and, yes,

a few will speak of cakes,
unsalted, on their tongues
offered as nourishment
or recompense for wrongs
by strangers strangely silent
who cover up their tracks —

Galactic travelers
who let their lives touch ours
while sojourning on Earth
. . . The stories may be true,
though cakes appear, too,
in folk and fairy myth,

where those who dare to taste
such food endure a spell
that robs them of their past,
all memory erased
— which does explain, at least,
how much they cannot tell.

A Word the Romans Used

The Latin word for poetry, carmen, *is also the word the Romans used for a song, a magic spell, a religious incantation, or a prophecy.*
— Dana Gioia

Carmen, the Latin word for poetry,
is the same word the Romans used for song.
My father Carmine played accordion —

His sisters called him "Carmen." Were they wrong
to hear his music as an incantation
off the beat, bound to a single key?

A magic spell, a song, a prophecy —
Each holds the power to lift us. For how long,
clouds breaking, did a dark sky hold the sun?

Was it a star in motion all along?
My father's namesake was Mount Carmel's vision —
Ailing, he kept her scapular nearby

useless without the right words. When he'd pray,
I'd think: *Words for the old or very young.*
"Carmen," his sisters smiled. They loved to listen,

Carmen, Carmine, Carmel on each tongue
that knew which name to speak or leave unspoken:
Mary, an apparition. Borne away,

the bellows resting on his knee, he'd sway
— Who were these women she was blessed among?
Each word a child speaks puts stars in motion

or, twice-blessed, they stay where they belong . . .
Words bring the charm, become the talisman
that summons *Carmen*, prayer, and poetry.

My Millay

Miss Caroline Dow, a woman of means . . . suggested a plan
to send Vincent to Vassar, naming several wealthy friends who
would be willing to put the plan into action.
— Daniel Mark Epstein

Our view originates in photographs,
her green eyes glinting gray above a smile
detached, flirtatious: girl and *poetess*,

archaic word more so applied to her,
sexual tempest with a Pulitzer —
Or maybe Steepletop in Austerlitz —

tree-rimmed, the ruined artesian swimming pool
whose water was acquainted with her skin;
the frayed books shelved in her "withdrawing room" —

Are these what come to mind? Is she the sum
of women and men she slept with, charmed, let go,
or kept as lifelong friends-with-benefits?

The chronic sufferer whose pain was eased
then caused by gin and morphine? (Married life
brought some relief: her Eugen paid for all,

discreet, devoted even in eclipse . . .)
Or is she — years before the next world war
pricked her to patriotism — the blinding star

who shared her bed with two men but divided
at the waist which pleasures each would know?
From Camden waif to goddess of Greenwich Village,

which view is true? Horse breeder, suffragette,
widow and recluse, racetrack gambler, muse?
I only know who comes to mind for me —

That girl — impoverished, costumed Pierrette,
red-blonde and ruffled, singing "Humoresque"
before the wealthy doyennes gathered round

the Whitehall Inn's new music room piano,
guest of the sister waiting tables there —
Proud autodidact, lauded for an encore

of the "Renascence" she knows by heart,
two hundred lines — the soul can split the sky —
soon to appear in print, as one grande dame

sits back and smiles, a plan about to form
— There are patrons to sway, a mother to persuade,
a girl whose gifts require benevolence.

Choose Your Adventure

What kind of traveler are you?
— Colorado tourist guide quiz

1. Start Here

Are you a very adventurous person?

Not very. Risk is something I avoid.
I watch the traffic on its slow advance
toward crosswalks empty of pedestrians . . . .
The flashing countdown makes me paranoid.

Are you afraid of heights?

The airships of the past
float, gleaming, through the sky
inflammable and blessed,
inviolate and gray.

Would you rather shop or read?

My currency is words: they buy me time,
each page a fraction of my fortune's worth.
Interest accrues with every borrowed rhyme —
They multiply, encircling the Earth.

Do you like to be a part of the action?

The action follows *me.* Another witness
casts the dice and bets against the reckless,
wrong, and dissolute, but finds more solace
in a stranger or an empty glass.

What's your favorite accessory?

My constant companion, my familiar,
tiger-striped shadow, sentry lost in sleep,
snow-throated occupier of low terrain
who stakes his claim by kneading common ground,
thumbed stalker of crumpled post-it notes and bedclothes,
vigilant thief on watch for signs of life.

Are you an athletic person?

The skeleton beneath my skin
emerges from its cage of flesh,
triumphant, till the wind returns
to sift the bones from dust and ash.

2. Your Results

The Adventure Junkie

You're not afraid of anything! For you,
"good times" depend on how fast you can go!
The Garden of the Gods waits at the summit —
You see yourself on top from far below.

The Retail Enthusiast

That Duchess on the wall is not your last —
You're a genuine Retail Enthusiast.
Your legacy's sure to enrich your sons.
Check out that god and seahorse cast in bronze!

The Fun Fanatic

You'll ride a railway straight up to the sky
because it's fun. You'll sky-dive just for laughs
then look for standing stones or cenotaphs —
There's pleasure in surviving history.

The Intellectual

Igneous rock, from magma formed,
speak now: was anybody harmed?
The cavern stream is crystalline,
but you're afraid of jumping in —
Confirm its source, and then: begin.

The Photographer

What do you see? The burnt magnesium
burns dark away till everything goes dark —
From tintype soldiers' torn-up uniforms,
iconic faces, kin, and Kodak kids,
(the world a splendid backdrop for their deeds)
to lost trails, mountain views, ghost town museums
waiting years for you to capture them
and turn your back. Before you've made your mark,
time speeding faster than you ever thought,
unsure what you'll remember or forget,

you photograph what hasn't happened yet.

Fool's Elegy

*He was the kind of person who would pretend to do
something stupid to make people laugh.*
                    — Brother of the 22-year-old who died July 4,
                       2015 in Maine after trying to launch
                       fireworks off the top of his head.

Peony, chrysanthemum, and willow —
bursts of color flung from aerial shells
across the night sky — filled his eyes, the thought
that he could make this night one to remember
quietly taking hold, though no one knew.
It had to be a joke, friends later said —
Not that they were entirely surprised,
cold beers tossed back in darkness, bottles lobbed
to thump in bins, while far-off neighbors led
the charge from parks and backyard barbecues.
Anything for a laugh — was that his motto?
You don't know how far's too far till you try.
And so his turn would come: to shine, brightly,
before the guys who, shocked, would stare struck dumb
in disbelief at his display of daring,
then dissolve in three cheers and applause.
The boys set off some fireworks of their own
as charcoal-embers faded on the grill,
the sky all noise; a girl brushed back her hair,
her bracelet's dolphin-charm catching the light,
and everyone advised, "That's crazy, man" —
young faces shadowed in midsummer gloom,
the porch light dim. If fame was close at hand,
he wouldn't find it standing in the yard

or with the charred duds smoking on the lawn,
but far above, the sea of stars so deep
that you could drown in it.
                              "Guys, check this out!"
he called, the mortar steadied on his head,
the fuse lit, sizzling as its core burned down
exactly as he'd planned. Eyes shut, he saw
what he alone was sure would happen next:

The night sky filled with flowers that boomed and glittered.
The shell launched safely in a shower of sparks
while he stood, singed, illuminated, alive —

No joker now, and braver than them all.

deadbook

For all your post-life social media needs

Reluctantly, I opened an account
sooner than I'd expected or desired.
You won't believe how many friends I found,
requests backed up. No password was required.

The latest status updates bring surprises
decades out of date; a few are sad.
I scroll the page, absorbed. A comment rises
then descends on some eternal thread.

I wouldn't say I like the conversations,
although I'd feel much worse if there were none.
I post replies, then wait, a slight impatience
stirring . . . . Is someone out there? Anyone?

At first, I felt relieved to find my profile
looked complete the moment I logged in,
but why can't I update it? In a while,
I'll click on "Help" and, maybe, try again.

I'm told the site is free and always will be.
Still, I feel unsettled, slightly lost . . .
Is nothing tangible? Who's listening, really?
Why should I care if strangers like my post?

— Yes, there are strangers here. We're not all friends.
Somehow, the long day's twilight never ends.
I tap the keys; there's nothing else to do.
It won't be long before I friend you, too.

To Genesis and Back

Grass was not they say. Fish were not they say. Deer were not then they say. Elk were not they say . . . . It was very dark.

The Cahto invocation of the past
began with naming what did not exist.
The world was empty, dark. No stars, no mountains,

nor the grass where deer poked and grazed —
No deer at all, in fact; no bears or crows,
no fish that gleamed below the water's surface . . .

And yet, the old chant summoned back so much —
the fox's scurry through the underbrush,
thrush-song, lush notes of larks and orioles . . .

To name what wasn't there restored it all,
symbolically, to tribal consciousness.
No Cahto Indian, I think of this —

Creation's re-creation ritual
long handed down, transcribed by passing linguists
at the dying of a native tongue

a hundred years ago. I think of those
whose heritage it carries, and of us,
enacting our own ritual of praise

and elegy, helpless to slow its pace —
A naming that precedes the vast erasure
Cahto ritual could not conceive.

So many noises — beasts and birds and insects,
audible to anyone who listened —
silent now. *Our* ritual is empty —

It goes on (we say) against our will,
but nothing happens when we speak the names.
The Cahto ritual reminded all

of what was absent prior to Creation,
offering its litany of lives —
screech-owls, condors, ravens, elk, coyotes —

creatures whose flesh and spirit *are* the world,
and who, beholding them, would not feel awed?
I've no claim on its mystery, nor words

for all the species lost or soon to be —
but helplessly, like you, I speak the names
in praise and elegy — ibex and rhino,

tiger and macaw — a waste of breath,
as if remorse could summon back their world,
or stay our hand and halt the vanishing

we mourn and cause, that beckons dead ahead —
A Genesis subtracted down to silence
as in its beginning, at its end.

Glory-of-the-Seas

This cone shell, Conus gloria-maris *Chemnitz, 4-5 in.*
long, is considered the most valuable shell in the world.
        — Sea Shells of the World, Golden Press,
        1962 edition

Once considered a great rarity, the Glory-of-the-Seas was a
much sought-after cone and thought to be the most valuable
shell in the world.
        — Sea Shells of the World, Golden Press,
        1985 edition

Glory-of-the-Seas, your name alone
would flourish still without your graceful whorls
and surface finely etched, exquisite cone
shell tenantless, more fabulous than pearls.

Better, you'd have brought in twelve hundred bucks
in '60s dollars if I'd found you beached
upon Long Island shores, emerged from flecks
of foam retreating swiftly. If I'd touched

you then, a boy, and held you in my palm,
fine gold thread-patterns mesmerizing me,
I'd have felt chosen, thrilled yet strangely calm,
destined for anything. How large the sea

that held you I could not conceive . . . . You lost
your luster in that decade's final year
when scuba divers swimming deeper, deepest,
found your habitat, unknown frontier

where, cast off, you lay numberless . . .

                                  Today,

I know the Philippines is far away,
the market's flooded, glory is no more,
and rare shells don't just wash up on the shore.

East of Tin Pan Alley

For Larry Cennamo,
Commack, Long Island, ca. 1965-1967

On blank staff paper, five lines parallel,
each named for letters that invoked my creed —
Every Good Boy Does Fine — I drew the circle
(whole note), filled it in: what did I need?
One stem called up a quarter note; connect
it to another, and I had an eighth.
Page after page I wrote. Could I expect
to sight-read soon? I'd struggle, take a breath,
and labor till my mother gave the word.
Mr. Cennamo, what was it you heard

each week, when I returned? My fingers blistered,
anxious, I'd hunch over my guitar,
whole body tensed after half-hours sequestered
with Mel Bay, decoding every bar.
In those first weeks, you stuck some masking tape
beside the tuning pegs, a flat drawn on,
so that, in doubt, I'd secretly look up
to see that flats meant, *Play a half step down.*
My mother sat nearby without a word.
Mr. Cennamo, what was it you heard?

In your split-level home, garage transformed
into your lair and warehouse, trumpets hung,
tarnished, along the wall. Unduly harmed,
a slideless trombone, old guitars unstrung
lay on the workbench. Studying the score,

plectrum in hand, painstakingly I'd play,
wishing, sometimes, I'd practiced even more,
not always sure I'd found the melody.
You sat beside me, offering some word
that gave me hope, at least. What had you heard?

Your own songs, scored by hand in India ink
straight from the Big Band age, on blank staff paper
marked and measured? "So, what do you think?"
you asked, playing us one, the strings' cool quiver
underneath your right hand echoing.
Your black hair, going gray, was neatly trimmed.
My mother, awed, gave praise. You placed the song
back on its stack, almost as if ashamed.
Was it a tune that someone might record,
someday? You didn't know . . . . One day, I heard

something like music issue from my guitar —
my mother turning from the stove to listen
while I practiced. Had I come so far
in so few months? Each week, another lesson,
punished fingers, and some standard stripped
down to its basics by yourself, or Mel,
brought me a little closer as I crept
toward mediocrity — though who could tell
what more might follow if I kept my word?
"Good boy," you said days later, when you heard.

II.

I heard telephones, opera house, favorite melodies . . .
                                        — "Five Years," David Bowie

Musicology

For Prince Rogers Nelson

What boy or girl, standing at the keyboard
after class, hears music no one's playing,
caught in memory? The risers wait,
ready for chorus members to line up.
Sand blocks and sleigh bells lie at rest until
tomorrow's class, and yet this black piano —
electric, digital — pulses with power,
still plugged in, screen aglow. What girl or boy —
untrained, used to the old cacophonies
that classmates bang out when the teacher leaves —
resists the urge or heeds some other call?
Who *hears* something and has to let it out?
The period's over, everybody's gone —
Ethereal xylophones, their voices muted,
lie beside their mallets in a box;
stacked tambourines, untouched, produce no sound —
And so, because you gave so much to many
through your songs, sweat-soaked performances,
dance moves a blur, medleys falsetto-drenched
through funky breaks and shouted ribaldries —
and, more: an artist moved to charity
who shared his largesse with those most in need,
anonymously, you made sure this boy
or girl, or any classmate here, could pause
within the haven of his solitude,
keep listening, draw near the instrument,
and gently bring one finger to the keys
to capture what might soon have disappeared,

unheard: the fragment of some favorite song?
The scattered notes that, rescued, form a tune
brand new? The chorus soon to start rehearsal,
tromping down the halls, will bring their noise,
chaos, and teasing with them, though for now
this girl, or boy, persists in listening,
alone but changed, the overtones just summoned
with the last note ringing still, alive
in mind and ear, the world enlarged somehow
as all that you've awakened slowly stirs.

Belated Aubade

This morning, "A Sunday Smile" played from the clock
beside our bed, shade drawn against the sunlight,
green walls swimming with aquatic shadow,
summer heat. The world was undersea,
alive and waiting, though we kept away
just then — it would be too much to endure —
and there was nothing more we asked of it,
except each other: gold hair on a shoulder
you could rest against; enough good luck
to last the day; brass, mandolin, and cello
half-heard, half-dreamt to the weary vocal
of a young man not yet half our age,
Jacques Brel-bravado summoning the courage
to seduce us while he says farewell.

Live from the Dakota

December 8, 1980

Through noise and smoke-haze drowning the TV
above the bar, your photograph flashed on
that Monday night close to semester's end
as if you'd joined the dead, closed captions still
unheard of as I glanced up at the screen.
Some file shot — outmoded mop-top, grin —
What were you up to now? But then the years —
your birth and death — appeared. I stood there, stunned,
proved wrong, but brought the brimming pitcher back
to friends for whom you held no special place —
Could that be true? It was. Still, they were kind
enough to hear me out, surprised as well.

What did I feel? The whirl of punk and disco
winding down had dropped me at the brink
of some new age I'd welcome or resist
to no avail, while you, five years retired,
were someone that I'd learned to live without.
Back briefly, twice as old, you were gunned down
before I'd yet forgiven you for leaving.
And who was I, exactly?
                              Poured beer banked
off empty glasses, Donna Summer mourned
a cake left under storm-clouds, while the Stones,
savvy survivors, vowed that they'd refuse
the role of burdened beast beneath the beat . . .

Back in my room, my girlfriend flipped through *Time*.
A record spun. I watched, blurred spectrum swirling
as the stylus fell, calling your voice —
loss-haunted, lasting — back into the world.

The Afterlife of Beatles

I like to think — dare I suggest, "imagine?" —
that, since Heaven holds eternity,
even those souls who fought to keep their rage in
here on earth calm down eventually.
I think of John: top cat and caustic leader,
rhythm guitarist, wag, satiric wordsmith —
during rehearsals, unrelenting needler
loved and feared by those he tangled with.
He joined George at the Maharishi's ashram,
Paul and Ringo, too; but, disillusioned,
stormed out, "He's no holier than I am,"
angry to hear the guru, drunk or stoned,
seduced an actress on the same retreat.
No more for John. The yogi's power was great,
        but so was his defeat:
George, too, packed up, swayed by the innuendo
swirling through the camp, his open window.

That George chose meditation as the way
to calm and clarity is no surprise:
he worked for John and Paul, assigned to play
the classic solos both would criticize.
The night his dentist spiked the sugar cubes
for after-dinner coffee, George and John
panicked to find the world transformed into
bright flame that lapped the road they drove upon.

His acid days behind him, the sitar's
consuming challenge finally given up,
George wrote his best songs, bent the slide guitar's
high weeping to his will. Should he bring up
his song allotment on the next LP?
He did, then sped home, angry in his Mini —
        "They can't decide on *any*?" —
Lank-haired, mustachioed, devout believer
tired of slights, the price of Beatle-fever.

Now he's gone, too. We've only Paul and Ringo —
extraordinary bassist and control freak
fluent in Scouse-slang and the boardroom's lingo,
and the sad-eyed, sickly child weakling
who grew up to steady the Beatles' beat.
A Knight widowed, remarried, Paul makes music,
driven to keep the faith, perhaps create
one track or two per album with the kick
of those he wrote in youth. Sometimes he does.
Ringo makes records, too, to pay the bills,
face masked by shades, soothed by the distant buzz
of L.A. from his mansion in the hills.
Two men who both seem slightly out of place
in our own time, despite a famous face —
        as if the carapace
of their identity could ever crack . . .
Irrationally, we want our Beatles back,

but John and George knew better. In the end,
one proud to call himself an atheist
rejected his own myth, let go our hand,
and sang, "The afterlife does not exist,"

the better to engage the world we know
for what good we can do. His songs got worse.
The other — part-time gardener, full-time Hindu,
ukulelist, self-proclaimed Dark Horse —
meditated on the ancient Vedas,
finding in their hymns a fiery cosmos
shining with the forces that create us,
All are one. Love all its highest Logos.
If Heaven belongs to Krishna, Christ, no one,
whatever its form — white island bleached by sun
        or Cavern mocked by John —
who knows what kind of afterlife we'll earn?
Two men: both seekers. Neither will return.

Charlie and The Beach Boys

McNeil Island Prison, Washington state, 1966

How did it feel to stand on deck, paroled,
a free man on the ferry to the mainland,
not knowing you'd find yourself, within a year,
living with Dennis Wilson of The Beach Boys
and your girls in sunny California,
strumming your songs, the dream within your grasp?
(Two girls hitchhiking on the Sunset Strip —
your girls — would give occasion to connect.)
How did it feel to watch the dream turn sour,
the demo sessions stalled, Brian indifferent
to your off-key voice, the promised contract
still in limbo, Dennis bearded, bored,
your flower-child girls oblivious?
Those dials and switches gleaming on a console
someone else controlled would serve a song
that held your truth: *Submission is a gift,*
cease to exist, plus some love-bead clichés
Dennis would steal because you owed him money
and record, revised, with band and brothers.
By then, you'd moved to Spahn ranch, hangers-on
and homeless kids collecting like the sagebrush
blowing through a movie, always West,
to form a family, somehow, as you led them,
pimp and grifter, prophet of coming war,
through hash and haze . . . . But what else did you brood on,
delusions of grandeur fueled by LSD?
Maybe that day, still locked up in your cell,
a year before the Summer of Love and Haight-

Ashbury head shops shocked authority,
when, static-chewed, over the wobbly wavebands
of a cheap transistor radio
you heard the far-off voices of a world
unlike your own or any that you'd known —
where strangers — other people — might belong,
all blended vocals, organ, harmonies
grim guards might confiscate at any moment.
You thought, *That should be me out there who's singing,*
shaking up the world till it explodes,
and though you knew release was months away
but couldn't know whose lives you'd one day twist
or ruin or take outright, you hunched in, listening,
humming along with one thought in your head,
hair trimmed, clean-shaven: *Wouldn't it be nice?*

Full Circle

We're captive on the carousel of time . . .

It's not so strange to want to sweep away
the life you've always led and start again
as someone else: a girl in peasant blouse
and corn-silk hair, your lyrics poetry,
the folk guitar you dragged from gig to gig
the same one that you use to write your hits,
and everyone you've ever known, your fan.
But since you can't, I guess the next best thing's
to wake up one day and find out your mother's
someone you never met, a household name —
some actor or rock star forced to give you up
against her will, hoping to reunite.
What doors would open? Who would you be now?

I thought about this in my teenage years
a lot — not that my life was so unhappy.
My parents weren't so bad; I had nice things,
hung out with friends, kept secrets, told the truth
if forced to, dated boys, but knew the fun
would end the way it did for everyone,
the same small voice discouraging us all,
Give up, get married, reproduce, and die.
I guess we all go through that phase, our parents'
lectures wasted as we roll our eyes.

What's strange is that the fantasy came true —
just not for me. It took me by surprise,
paging through *People* on the checkout line,

my boy a toddler, restless, small legs kicking
through the grocery buggy's metal cage
when, suddenly, it all came flooding back —
The endless days that ended after all,
the record player I unsnapped like luggage
after school upstairs when I got home,
the albums like a giant tarot deck
spread out to tell my fortune on the rug:
One day, Neil Young will carry you away.

Joni, you had a child at twenty-one.
You were the thing we feared we could become —
Dirt-poor in a Toronto rooming house,
a girl without a home, a single mom
back when you might as well have murdered someone
and been treated better. For a while,
some guy stepped in, the dad already gone,
but didn't stay, which made things even worse —
A child with a child pretending, like the song
we didn't know you wrote about yourself.
What could you do except give her away?
Still, I was envious: your daughter's life
was blessed and fortunate. If I'd been brought
up like her: spoiled, well off, a private school girl
used to gifts and tropical vacations
— If clues, old files, and accidents had proved,
after the dead ends of a five-year search,
somehow, I was the daughter of a star,
I'd have been shocked like her, yet level-headed,
thankful to live a fairy tale come true.

People makes these reunions sound so easy!
All parties were forgiving or forgiven,
the couple who raised her pushed to second place,
all willing to tie the loose ends in a bow
and smile from ear to ear, Joni absolved
and free, her daughter welcomed, radiant.
It didn't last, but that's another story.
The spotlight of celebrity is harsh
on those not used to living in its glare,
but who knows? Maybe they've made up by now,
I hope so, anyway . . . .
                              As for my son,
he's seventeen and sulks when I hold forth
and tell him, "Treat your girlfriends with respect!
Make sure they don't end up like —" Well, you know.
It's ten years since his dad and I divorced.
Should stories end when everyone gets old,
their wounds displayed or hidden in plain sight,
or at the Hallmark moment when their joy
shines brightest? Even Joni wasn't Joni
in her youth, just one more pregnant girl
struggling to hold and strum her instrument,
shut in a room, afraid to call her parents,
and I was me — not her, and not her daughter —
only a teenage girl lost in music
like my friends, the words we sang inscribed
on notebooks, three-ring binders, fortune tellers.
We rode that carousel, hoping that when
the music stopped, we'd step off in a world
where what we felt while carried off by song
was what we'd feel forever: touched, transformed
into the someone else we truly were.

The Ghosts of Thunder Road

There are ghosts in the eyes of all the boys you sent away.
They haunt this dusty beach road in the skeleton frames
of burned-out Chevrolets . . .

You're lucky. You know the reason you were born —
to get away, no matter what it takes —
whatever the cost in lies or broken lives,
to run and keep on running till the road
straight into the sun dissolves into a future
where you crash, and both of you are free.
I'm not, and never will be. I'm the ghost
who lingers near the highway in the eyes
of boys and men sent broken-hearted, gut-punched,
into the night by someone who once loved them,
thought she did, or said so at the time,
then, suddenly, found crow's feet at the corners
of her eyes and flooded with regret.
Regret's a funny thing. I stand here now —
frail wisp of cigarette smoke, just a shadow
waiting at the curb where gravel sprays —
and everything is different, yet the same:
boys come and go, or disappear like me,
unless they move on or turn into men
she tolerates a while, then sends away.
Things don't work out. Years pass, back roads and turnpike
filling with faster rigs and newer cars —
Then you show up, all promises and smooth talk,
with your ax and catalogue of conquests:
Wendy, Rosey, Janey, Bobby, Terry
who shared the squalor of your squatter's beach house,

Mary, and dozens more who shared the name
that summer and beyond.
                              It's her name, too —
my Mary, the one who sits out on her porch
at summer's end and hears the crickets dying
in the brush, or men behind the wheel
on streets of fire where sirens whirl and fall.
I listen to your trash talk — watch and learn
what doesn't do a ghost much good to know,
past pleasures of the flesh seared off the bone
in one last fiery wreck or blaze of glory —
Take your pick. The ending is the same.
For you, the world's a highway freshly paved,
where men flee cops, the darkness in themselves,
though you'll fly past them, wrapped in legs and leather
on your hog, or drive on in your car,
windows rolled down and losers left behind —
Will Mary join you, or stay back with them?
A choice is made. She smiles. I'd feel betrayed
if ghosts could feel a thing except indifference,
pity past love, and glimmers of contempt
for soothing words that stroke, and close the deal.
How can an insult make her want you more?
She *is* a beauty — *was* one, anyway —
but now I watch her stand behind the screen,
haloed in porch light as she nears the door
to touch you through the mesh — a touch so brief
I might have missed it if the touch of flesh —
transient, chaste — were one I'd know again.
Go to him, Mary. Right now. No regrets.
Step down, the screen door swinging as you rush
from porch to car into whatever future

endless highways, bars, and beach roads hold
for this New Jersey Romeo, leather-clad
in his Camaro, where a beat-up Fender
waits, responding to his touch, or not —
as you will till the day that he's betrayed
you yet again with Wendy, Rosie, Janey,
or another Mary on the beach,
while Tillie, painted host upon the Palace,
smiles in jest or pity...
                              Or maybe not —
Maybe a hoodlum *is* your best escape
from faded tassels hung on rear view mirrors,
battered high school bleachers, roadhouse nights,
time's etching on your face . . . . One thing I know:
I'll be here waiting when you come back home
alone, or not — when every other ghost
who's lost someone or gotten lost himself
emerges from barren woods to stand and watch,
waiting like me, with me, heartless and young,
dreaming of life, in awe of what it holds,
while winter once more grips the park and boardwalk,
pedal boats clutched in ice against the dock,
the neon off, the Ferris wheel shut down,
bright snow descending through its frozen frame.

Tinker to Evers to Chance

For Scott Miller, founder of Game Theory
and The Loud Family

Tinker to Evers to Chance: so fortune bears us,
spinning, like a hundred-year-old baseball
into nothingness, the double play
from short to second to Uncertainty —
the final stop, dropped ball, or awful moment
when we know what must abruptly follow,
helpless to do anything but watch.

Forever, we think, *there's a chance*: we hope for grace,
the California kind your songs delivered —
sun-scorched, timeless, filled with girls' names
(that old songwriter's trick), each name a spell
that fired a synapse — sing out, *Shalini*
(or *Sheila*, et al.) — every ex- a why
that, real or not, you searched ingeniously,

as if rethinking every choice or chance
through words sung in the "miserable whine"
you called your vocals too self-critically.
At Gabe's Oasis, live, frontman of five,
you rose above the dive's din like more tinder
fire-drenched, spent; your solo encore followed,
fearless, ardent — pickups rang and hummed,

blonde Telecaster burning with the chance
to test the boundaries of the mixing board.
Spin, Billboard, Rolling Stone: the critics loved

you — fans, too, though too few; labels collapsed,
no one got rich, while dazzling melodies
struck through your songs like lightning, harmonies
that brightened youth, our backward century.

Tinker to Evers to Chance: "Their names," you said,
"evoke so many meanings, and they kept
players from getting hits: the perfect title
for our farewell compilation disc."
(Such pop-foul fragments of pop history
you scattered through your songs.) You paid the bills
working in Silicon Valley. When you died,

surrendering yourself to chance forever,
one of the daughters you left fatherless
approached your stricken widow with a likeness
crude in crayon — "Don't cry, Daddy's here" —
to stop her mother's tears, but in the stream
of data, CDs burned or bought, the chords
and words you left us all, they'll find you, too.

Season of Elliott

For Elliott Smith

The steering wheel reverses in my hands,
the turn resolved, the traffic's give-and-take
in swift retreat, thin trees where nothing lands
blown back in warm wind as if soon to break
in amber light this summer afternoon
not cool, not hot, the color of the moon
(smashed light bulb) spreading fast if we look far
enough, beyond the bypass and the car
that carries us to where we disappear
from friends who grieve, though we know where we are —
The season of Elliott is drawing near,

season of Alphabet City tenements,
crushed vials in gutters, strange beds where we wake
alone with thoughts of sudden accidents
sure to befall us stumbling down the track
through subway tunnels in a darkness strewn
with trash, remains of wrecked lives. Or, too soon,
the opposite: white suit, the blinding star
of spotlights and applause, and a guitar
so drowned by violins we hardly hear
its waltz-time strum behind the monitor —
The season of Elliott is drawing near.

It doesn't matter if the lead line bends
in thick distortion, memory leading back
to some unwanted stepdad who depends
on nightly beatings and surprise attack,

to force his will upon a borrowed son.
It doesn't matter if it was misfortune
for a mother, stranded and unsure
of what she really knew, to shut the door
on doubt, the better judgment of her fear.
What's real or not will end in metaphor —
The season of Elliott is drawing near.

It's making up a new name, one-night stands
of solo sets that feel like a mistake
when hecklers shout and drunks make their amends
by screaming out requests. It's feeling fake
with old friends, an imposter out of tune
with fans and hangers-on; it's needle, spoon,
and bliss after a long night at the bar;
it's finger-picking patterns soon to spar
with bass and drums, articulate and clear.
It's flowers offered to the warrior —
The season of Elliott is drawing near.

We feel it most at twilight, far from Portland's
Old Town where demolished clubs still quake
with ghosts and reverb; borne up by the winds
they call the Santa Ana as they rake
across L.A. from butte and desert-dune —
Winds hot and dry as these. Does every rune
on wall or street-sign, passing in a blur
say anything or lead us anywhere?
The knife's edge soon to follow the premiere —
The cane that spins a busker's hat forever —
The season of Elliott. Is drawing near

the same as drawing toward oblivion?
— As if in answer, dim at the horizon
where a stranger calls, "One more, one more,"
reluctant encores fade into the whisper
of a fragile voice, another year
some live to see and, driving on, remember —

The season of Elliott is drawing near.

Groovy Decay

In part because one Hitchcock was enough
though fascinated by *Groovy Decay*'s
display of candles, fruit, a skull in shades
("groovy" indeed), familiars in your photo
on the album's sleeve, I turned away,
your songs unheard, and bought, instead — who knows?
Probably something used, $3.95
the era's usual price for LPs crackling
with the noise of endless revolution,
dirty needles, dust. I'd haunt the aisles
of record stores, the best — Plastic Fantastic
on West Lancaster — pleased to accept
its cut of borrowed dollars guaranteed
by New York State, the law, my signature.
(The vinyl sold was guaranteed as well,
to play without a skip, or money back.)
I loved the album *1999*
in 1982, blaring from Bryn Mawr
dormitory windows as I walked
cross-campus to the white Victorian house
of Marxist scholars and medievalists
united in their shared distaste for me.
A grad school misfit marking time, adrift,
I couldn't quit — not yet. Where would I go?
At twenty-two, in that depression year
of AIDS and Reaganomics, I'd walk out
of class as if in search of some lost chord
that, struck, would resonate and break the mood

(I found that album in the "used" bin, too),
but nothing did. Not even the escape
of music, self-abuse, and poetry.
I'd pick through sleeves worn ragged at the edge,
split cardboard cracked — LPs *not* guaranteed,
so cheaper still — while clerks hippie-hirsute,
Cure-coiffed or Banshee-lashed took inventory,
ragged on new releases, or zoned out.
These dregs of discs I held up to the light
(it was allowed), checking for boot-scuffs, cracks,
carved messages to ex-friends, faithless lovers
who'd betrayed then asked for records back.
No one shook gloves with cardboard Michael Jackson.
Impishly imperial, Elvis stared
in straw hat, scowl, and granny spectacles
from posters masking-taped to sunlit windows
on a world where it would dawn on me —
not soon — that should the wrathful gods, appeased,
allow me to have sex again, someday,
I'd have to wear a condom, probably.

Robyn, you had a bad year, too, I know,
hating the "ghastly" saxophones your songs
were forced to bear, a studio of strangers
hostile to your retrodelic vision
and Syd Barrett squall. You hit the pubs
and shunned recording for the next three years,
convinced black grooves had caught the slow decay
of time and talent, though uncanny moments,
overproduced, still shone. The other Hitchcock
left us movies: fear, the body's weight,
detective work and doublings; small and large,

the soul's transgressions, love, the grave's embrace.
Like you, he'd have agreed: decay *is* groovy,
wicks burn down, wax melts, a certain skull,
blind-socketed, sports shades; meanwhile, you lift
your gaze to God or glory, Holy Ghost
or yellow logo: entropy takes hold,
and yet, though death's more probable than life
under the best conditions, we receive,
unearned, one second chance after another
till the count-in to the final set.
Gray-haired, past sixty, touring on your own
or with the Venus 3, you're writing songs
as good any in your long career,
and even I, somehow, escaped that year
of failure, pratfalls, and paralysis,
exiled in Pennsylvania, vinyl rippling,
warped, a diamond stylus drawing music
from the grooves it damaged as they spun
beneath its touch, the tone arm lifting off,
having reached silence, equilibrium.

As for your music, Robyn, I first heard it
six years later in a Midwest bar
locals had dubbed the "Miscue," billiards knocking
hard, percussively, across green felt.
"Who's *that?*" I said, raising my head to listen
in those pre-grunge days, through beer-mugs banging,
howls, and pick-up lines, while Doug sank balls,
deftly, into their pockets. Debra smiled,
and told me, cue beside her as we stood
waiting for Doug to miss. And miss he did,
finally, though open-mouthed through Debra's turn,

balls racked and struck, her black bob flung aside
with every shot, I looked up toward the speakers
from which poured the chords of "Chinese Bones,"
as if to make the song more audible,
more charged with loss than it already was.

Patti in Orbit

Vassar College Chapel, April 7, 1979

Patti, what was audible past the ceiling
beams of dark wood, terminal angels watching
from above, winged guardians halved & gilded
— "Space Monkey"'s feedback?

Fixed on high, celestially overhead, blank
faces stayed blank, glimmers of stage lights flashing
over us, your audience in the chapel —
Why were you awful?

You were high, too: obvious from your banter —
"Where are all the good-looking models?" "Fuck it,
I don't feel like reading tonight," your book slammed
shut as the band played

fiercely, stoned, too, "High on Rebellion" missing
half its text, the poem at its core & climax.
Strobe-lit Len, guitarist of poise & power,
drug-dazzled, soloed —

How high were *we* after such hype & clamor?
Were you crashing, spiraling downward fast, or
off course temporarily? "No, I'd never
play a gig just for

women; or play only for humans, either,"
you replied to stage-crowding hedonists. What
did my girlfriend — classically trained pianist —
think of this bedlam?

She took things in stride — a distinct advantage
at that time for anyone dating me. But
where was *he*, ape avatar, fueled & star-struck —
racing the night sky?

Patti, close to spinning away, you landed
safe & sober, marrying, in Detroit, Fred
"Sonic" Smith. Typed pages & more Smiths followed.
Raising a family,

music on hold — this was the life that saved you
& the choice that, later on, left you widowed,
fired with grief, inspired to resume recording —
After the fadeout

fades out, what's next? Mapplethorpe memoir, tributes,
time bearing down: Space Monkey high that evening
locked in Quaalude orbit beyond the solar
asteroid belt, or

radar-jammed, craft plunged in Pacific waters
sky-blue by day?
                                        Alien ape, lost pilot,
will we know you, simian gold & glowing,
when you appear?

Or will Patti summon you back to grimace
at the sight of what was but one more planet
on your journey, no more or less important,
when it's forgotten?

Major Tom and David Bowman

After "Space Oddity" and 2001: A Space Odyssey

What's the "oddity"
in David Bowie's song
about the astronaut
we know as Major Tom?
There's none: it's just a pun
on Kubrick's *Odyssey*,
inspired by the shot
of Frank Poole cast adrift,
unspooling into space
past any hope of rescue
from unending darkness,
betrayed by a computer's
dark intelligence.
So, too, will David Bowman
meet the same misfortune
unless the only voice
besides his own is silenced,
the vital key in hand,
each cartridge he removes
erasing memory,
regressing sentience
into a few short lines
of *Daisy, answer do*
eerily winding down.

But Major Tom, alone,
sounds unafraid, it's true.
The world below him spins
away his one last chance
to join its gravity —
Too late. The wife he loves
will never see him land.
His circuit dead, he's tensed,
prepared to make a choice.
Propelled from Earth and Sun
without much oxygen,
what does he feel — defiance?
Ground Control's intruders
matter less and less;
the earth below, still blue,
cloud-streaked, is now a place
he's permanently left,
this "tin can" all he's got
in all the galaxy
— But now that Earth is gone
for good, the steady hum
of static drowns all thought
of turning back, what's wrong
or right resolved: *I'm free.*

Star Child

Citizens of the universe, recording angels
We have returned to claim the pyramids
    — George Clinton

All right, Star Child, no longer Clarke's or Kubrick's,
you're the alien whose aim is wild
in 3D shades, bound for the stone where Hendrix
took flight, Star Child —

Do you recall which frequency you dialed,
what cosmic road you'll glide before you fix
your course on planet Earth & land, exiled

with souls whose rumble reached you, trading licks
so fine the gods of Easter Island smiled?
What subspace chatter, garbled in the mix,
called to the child

in us, Star Child? In you? If someone's hex
could summon lost ships from Bermuda's hold,
or cast spells locked in Egypt's hieroglyphics,
yours might, Star Child,

traversing light years, whirling disc unveiled
in lustrous lazy 8s that bend & flex
all starlit night. What secrets stand revealed

aboard your Mothership — in bass lines, sax,
& drums — to free our minds & leave us thrilled?
From Sun Ra, Jesus, Jimi to . . . Who's next? —
That's right: Star Child.

Rescuing the Voices

The story of the Langley sessions is . . . [the story of] how
a young rock guitarist, needing a job, became a gypsy
music teacher in a Canadian farm region and created
timeless recordings that were never intended to be heard
beyond the school community's perimeter.

You know the songs — "Space Oddity," "Good Vibrations,"
"The Long and Winding Road," a dozen more —
arranged for voice, percussion, xylophones,
performed by untrained children near Vancouver

during the 1970s, gathered together
from different rural schools to take positions
on the risers, facing the young conductor
who led them through "Space Oddity," "Good Vibrations,"

captured in Spector-sized echo, young musicians
filling the school gymnasium with fervor,
missing their notes in unison, expressions
rapt for "The Long and Winding Road," and more,

classics and corn, "Mandy" and "Wildfire"
sung into empty space: ideal conditions,
strangely, for making a record, the teacher's guitar
steadying voices, percussion, xylophones

pinging, mostly on cue, throughout the sessions
no audience but the children and their director
witnessed, caught in one take, the imperfections
of voices from the outskirts of Vancouver

pressed onto vinyl, forgotten. But their renditions,
rediscovered, survive. *You ain't gettin' no younger*
chorus gone silent, a soloist, past all questions,
sings to every desperate listener
who needs her song.

III.

Who are 'contingent faculty'? Depending on the institution, they can be known as adjuncts...non-tenure-track faculty, clinical faculty, part-timers, lecturers, instructors . . . . What they all have in common: they serve in insecure, unsupported positions with little job security and few protections for academic freedom. And they are the vast majority of US faculty today.

— American Association of University Professors (AAUP)

Then those who towered above the rest in intellect and bold
Imagination, day by day showed how to change the old
Manner of life with fire and new ways of doing things.

— Lucretius, *The Nature of Things*, A. E. Stallings, translator

Leya's Ghostly Cats

For a grad school classmate and longtime faculty colleague

Leya's ghostly cats resist the darkness
of the office where they sprawl, aglow,
upon my monitor, four luminous
translucent toys. But where is Leya now?
"She's in a better place," a friend suggests,
employing tact; and, yes, that much is true —
far from the gaze of grim antagonists
or plastic housecats fading out of view.

She found another job. It happened fast.
My sometime office mate and longtime colleague
finally got away, escaped the past,
the numbing plague of politics and intrigue.
The cats are one small kindness left behind,
oblivious, mute, but how much they'd have seen
if they'd crawled out and spied on us, resigned,
alive and phosphorescent, pale green.

A voice that whispers, *We don't need her here,*
She publishes too much. It shames us all.
I never got to sabotage her hire,
one more laments. *She's ready for a fall.*
One ghostly cat, tail high, stands at attention,
frozen in position, like the rest . . .
The final voice it sickens me to mention:
It's time that she was properly assessed.

In academia, is there a crime
more fraught with risk than to exceed your place?
The day news spread of Leya's Guggenheim
the trap was sprung. Lips curled, the faintest trace
of malice in a greeting coldly given
gave concern, but what could she have done?
Give back the grant, give up? The ghostly heaven
of the cats is not for everyone.

Not even twenty years and seven books
could rescue Leya, risen through the ranks
without the rights of tenure . . . . If no one looks,
then no one sees, and no one need give thanks.
The Powers-That-Be refused the unpaid year
that she requested to pursue her project.
The phosphorescent quartet fades, I fear,
denied the sun and dusty with neglect.

What made her vulnerable? Retirements, mostly:
hired in youth, we dared reach middle age.
Our tenured allies left, each loss more costly,
till we reached the turning of a page . . .
A small cat, phosphor-charged, feels no such envy
for his fellow lifeless ornaments,
nor will he turn on those arranged benignly
by his side, whatever the pretense.

But faculty are something else. The laughter
of a manic voice set free to rule
disrupts the hallway now and ever after
with pretended kindness that turns cruel.

My wife, long tenured, hangs on, terrorized,
unfireable, as cold eyes turn to me,
and plans take shape . . . I'm neutered, neutralized,
the glow I wear now fading rapidly.

. . . Well, Leya's gone. I'm here, just like the cats,
and other tokens tacked up on the board;
a handmade Christmas greeting; cards or notes
I save in books. With luck, I'll be ignored
a little longer here among small gifts
and keepsakes of the old days . . . Leya thrives
elsewhere, as she deserves. The darkness lifts.
Her cats grow dim, but one of us survives.

Gimpel the Adjunct

After Isaac Bashevis Singer's "Gimpel the Fool"

One day, after a period of mourning
for the colleagues who had been forced out
before me on some technicality
embedded in our contracts like a bomb,
the Spirit of Evil rose before my window,
passed through glass and, smiling, clicked his tongue.
"How can you sleep, Professor? Don't you know
that after twenty years your time's run out?
Though Frampol University once pledged
secure employment for a job well done,
today's contingent faculty are fired
on a whim. Get up and pack your things!"
I jerked awake, turned from the screen, and blanched,
my guest's sharp tail swinging impatiently.

It wasn't the first time he'd appeared here,
this Spirit of Evil, horned, goat-bearded, sly.
Faced with five first-year courses per semester,
stacks of grading, low pay, less respect,
I'd weakened, tempted by his murmured words,
"Why work so hard? Just offer empty praise —
Be *entertaining* — that's not hard for you —
Above all, don't dare challenge their beliefs
or cast in doubt their chance to get an A.
Your popularity will hit the roof!"
I'd wavered — but my students' faces hovered,
smooth or pimply, freckled, bright or dim,
kids far from home, eager to start new lives,
they'd turned to me. I couldn't let them down.

"I bet you wish you'd listened to me then,"
he hissed, his sharp teeth jagged in a grin
not quite a grin, persuasive as I saw
the junk that I'd collected through the years —
outdated syllabi, long-yellowed texts —
So much to pitch or save . . . But who'd save *me*?

I've never been a man to hold a grudge —
An orphan, I'm well practiced in acceptance
of the toil deserving people shun,
disparage, scoff at, then assign to me,
but when I thought back on the tales I'd heard
from provosts proud to claim benevolence,
I had to wonder: what did *they* believe?

— Gimpel, at Frampol University
everyone's valued, even you, despite
your lowly adjunct's pay; everyone's welcome
to speak freely here, though adjuncts' jobs
can blow away like smoke in seconds flat.
If someone you displease holds rank above you,
be assured: no one will act unkindly,
though due process isn't guaranteed.
Oh, and Gimpel — there's a fair in heaven,
A cow flew over the roof and laid brass eggs.
The dead have risen at the ram's horn blast —
Don't worry — your next contract's on the way.

— Suddenly, I felt capable of all
my sinister intruder might suggest
now that the veil was pulled from truth and lies —
"And yet, devil or dybbuk, should his will
rule mine?" I thought. "What waits beyond these walls,
this office not yet emptied, too soon filled

by younger adjuncts hired for even less?"
He heard: "What nonsense! Nothing waits for you —
No world to come, no job. Even your colleagues
safely tenured soon will find themselves
crushed by decrees enacted while they sleep."
That's when I left for good, last class be damned.
Whatever the Spirit of Evil had in mind,
I left him to pursue his noxious errands
skulking in the shade of other desks
where he could whisper new strategic plans —
tone-deaf pronouncements, layoffs, budget cuts
to deans who bow before the bottom line
that rules their faith and sets their conscience free.

As for me, what's past is like a dream
glimpsed from a bed of straw . . . From town to town
I wander the world, chalked blackboards half-erased,
in search of purpose, parking, office space,
young faces baffled, blank yet listening
as I spin tales, outlandish words, strange things

but — God be praised — I cannot be deceived.

Animal College

Somehow it seemed as if the farm had grown richer without making any of the animals themselves richer — except, of course, for the pigs and the dogs.
— George Orwell, *Animal Farm*

Why are there so many Dogs and Pigs
among the deans and trustees at the top?
When did they learn to walk upon two legs?
What work absorbs them? Will they ever stop

e-mailing the edicts that fill up their days?
Would having power seem pointless otherwise?
What programs will they next reorganize,
downsize, or slash? And yet, we nap and graze,

Faculty Sheep, who quarrel over scraps,
bleating for more while waiting to be sheared . . .
What flatteries lie trembling on our lips,
seeking approval, straining to be heard

by Canines whose replies consist of "facts"
and PowerPoints of prescience and precision?
Tenure is obsolete. Come, share our vision —
MOOCS for the mob, tech-generated texts,

and porcine deals sealed by a wink and handshake —
These are the future. Must one more stadium
rise up while Boars and Barkers call, *Awake!*
Enrollment's dropped! and other tedium

that keeps the flock off balance, on all fours?
Increase class size! Impose a salary freeze! —
When squeals and howls expose the sympathies
of those who profit while tuition soars,

whose Greater Good is served? More corporate kiosks,
raises for Hogs and Hounds, a Five-Year Plan
whose bullet points raise questions no one asks —
and for those sheepish creatures who remain,

high course loads and resigned obedience . . .
Do Dogs and Pigs sleep soundly in the knowledge
that to serve them is to serve the College?
A few lost Sheep could tell the difference, once.

From an Exile in Auden's Time

Beyond the vacant *-isms* of the day
that you resist in any age or era
lies a wilderness where what you say
is wrong — dead wrong — and must be met with Power,

silenced, or conjoined to some idea
that discredits you with all the error
of its shameful practice. Mercy's shown
only when you're irrelevant, or gone,

or willing to concede, when duly pressed,
what you believe you saw you never witnessed.
Power is good and acts with Good in mind —
the larger, public good. Its face is kind,

suffused with light and clarity of vision,
resolved to impose freely, without restraint,
its willful, absolute Imagination
toward a better world. Because you can't.

Give in: survival's better than salvation.
Your conscience isn't clear; nobody's is.
Unwelcome truths will only sow division . . . .
To say more would be pointless, perilous.

A Leader for Our Times

He knew human folly like the back of his hand . . .
— Auden

He said the things we didn't know we felt —
hard truths that showed us what we really feared,
and whom. We listened as he lifted guilt
from our collective conscience. What we heard
reached to the core, though each of us heard something
different that convinced us he was right.
We heard, beyond our borders, rumbling —
Within our borders, reason taking flight.
It felt like freedom. In our neighbors' eyes
we saw a common light, or signs of doubt
that marked the enemies he'd brutalize,
the former friends we'd learn to live without . . .
His jokes amused us, booming from the stage —
We dreaded — and looked forward to — his rage.

Crybully

Crybully never hits. He hits you *back*.
He's got to. You spoke out, and started it.
You're wrong again, he's happy to admit.
He'll tell you so before your next attack,

which he'll insist is anything you say.
Don't show them any weakness is his motto.
Crybully's favorite tactic is bravado.
He punches hard, so get out of his way!

Does he apologize? What do you think?
He spits out answers, fully automatic.
If speech were radio, he'd be the static.
He'll trip you with a handshake and a wink,

then tell the world you brought it on yourself.
Crybully know no limits except yours.
Are you the vacuum that his power abhors?
He read a book once, tossed it on the shelf,

but still remembers some of what it said —
Something about a big lie, or the rate
at which the gullible may procreate —
(*A minute: that's one more!*) . . . . And yet his dread,

shameful and dark, is obvious to all —
The whole world's ganging up on him again!
In victory, he'll prove the better man
by jailing the vanquished as they fall —

Crybully's sure of this, and other things:
The whole world envies him, including you.
He'll touch and grab you if you want him to,
or if you don't. That's how it is with kings,

and why Crybully follows you around.
He hears you talking calmly, and he seethes
self-righteously, or roars, sniffs when he breathes.
He'll deafen us before you make a sound,

destroy your life and family, burn your town
because you stood your ground and met his gaze.
Crybully even scares his friends these days,
but will he lift a finger when they drown?

Dream Songs for the Governor of Michigan

1.
Why is our boiled water brown?
Our bottled water's running out.
Will it be safe to drink again?
Why shouldn't water touch our skin?

The water mains still underground
belong to a forgotten age —
The records we've retrieved so far
don't always point to where they are,

and, yes, we have a deficit —
which means we can't repair them yet.
But rest assured: your water's safe.
True, there are problems with its taste,

color, and smell, but samples show
lead levels are extremely low.
We hear you. We've conducted tests.
The wheels of government are slow.

2.
When water from the tap won't clear —
When families forced to cook with it
get sicker, do we share their rage?
Or do we share in their defeat

when hydrants flush the streets metallic
orange — one more tainted purge?
When residents desperate to sell
are turned away by realtors?

Water, once thought a public good,
is now one more commodity:
expendable, like those who live
in devastated neighborhoods.

3.
Why change a city's water source
to one inarguably worse?
You know why: it was cheaper. Summer
days, pools fill with teenage swimmers,

laughter, lead. How soon will daughters,
showering, watch hair fall out
in clumps that catch in rusted drains?
How will the elderly, the poor

assured it's safe, protect themselves?
Stop washing when their rashes burn?
Or let caregivers sponge their flesh —
the toxic river's toxic touch.

We know this water's poisonous.
Who'll stop or redirect its course?
We're told we have to wait. How long?
Who's listening, if anyone?

4.
Hair white, startled from sleep, a man
who should have known pads down the stairs,
thirsty. What does he see at night?
Iced-over windows, mandalas

of frost on glass. He pours and drinks —
fresh water from the faucet, cool
and clear: the least that he deserves.
What do the least of Michigan

deserve from those responsible?
If citizens are customers
and nothing more, then, yes, they're lost.
What should they ask this Governor,

and others like him? *Shouldn't water
wash us clean and nourish life?
Who sent this poison to our homes,
as if to kill or scatter us?*

Don't turn your back in disbelief.

Confidential Report on the State of the Empire

Intercepted intelligence briefing originating abroad, ca. 2016

Few opportunities present themselves
at first glance, to the casual observer.
But take a closer look. The public smile
they wear behind the counter or the desk —
false cheer to face a future that they fear —
betrays a helplessness they can't conceal,

and so, we cannot help but feel for them,
so wrong, sadly misguided in their myths
. . . Not that pity weakens our resolve.
How do they live? Distracted by their toys,
intrusive ads that promise new toys soon,
they trade their privacy for taking pictures

with the phones that track their every move,
and nothing's real unless it's photographed.
(We photograph them, too, and listen in.
They don't care. That's how passive they've become.)
Unmoored, they praise or mock the candidates
they vote for or against, celebrities

who spark disdain instead of empathy —
That's key: the loss of empathy, I mean.
Both young and old lash out — in life, on-line —
on impulse, as if any point of view
besides their own is deeply dangerous —
(In this respect, I guess, they're much like us.)

And these, remember, are the lucky ones,
occupied, employed. Others, worse off,
are everywhere and have no voice at all.
Deprived of shelter, jobs, tempered by loss,
they're ready to tear down the palaces —
The least that we can do is lend a hand.

What holds them back? Not much: the rule of law.
Still, times have changed. They looked for heroes, once.
Now they're on watch for defects, further proof
no one should govern them; that laws, like men,
too flawed to be obeyed, deserve their scorn
(and when they earn high office, women, too).

What brought them to this point is hard to say.
In God We Trust clings to their currency,
though few believe. The rest believe too much —
They're sick of terror, constant vigilance
against a world that sees through their pretense,
and crave release, whatever form it takes,

driven to engineer their own demise,
believing that technology, somehow,
will lift them up, restore preeminence,
the glories of a bygone century,
and generate a hefty profit, too.
How is it possible they're so naïve! —

To think a global web so easily breached
could keep them safe, protect their power grids,
ensure defense, the safety of their skies
. . . I guess it's innocence, a childlike impulse
to believe the past won't pass away,
but, no. It's not our place to calm their fears —

A. Pope?

85

Our job is to remain professional.
Like children lost, they fight among themselves
which frees us to proceed . . .

But when they fall,
as soon they will, I think I'll miss them most
not for the twilight they inhabit now
but for their total faith that they were called —

destined, it once was said — to lead the world.

Text and Flame

The news brings such terrible stories —
The girl who kept texting a friend
to give up the weight of his worries,
and bring his own life to an end.
The woman who fought against fire
found dead in a national park,
shamed in an unending furor —
A rescuer lost in the dark.

Why do we still feel distant
the more every distance is bridged?
Devices — pervasive, insistent —
might bring us together, as pledged,
and yet, we adapt to their medium,
our avatars shifting and small,
our voices turned text, or turned tedium?
And are we much closer at all?

That girl at the mall, half-distracted,
her friends cracking jokes as she smiled,
kept texting the boy, undetected,
words flashing between them. She dialed —
Depressed, he was weak or unwilling
to take the last step and grow up —
No one could confuse this with killing —
She texted him finally: *Time's up.*

A woman who's called to fight fires
should keep her true feelings in check,
or else the regard she inspires
will change to abuse or attack —
anonymous, crude — that pursues her
on-line in chat forums that seethe
with rumors that hang there forever,
unproven, until she can't breathe —

The firemen on duty beside her
(or strangers who sounded like them)
had mocked her failed marriage and tied her
to multiple partners, her name
ridiculed out in the open —
harassment she lived with for weeks.
What were we expecting to happen?
The Web forgives no one's mistakes.

When did the world that we live in,
intangible, wireless, unreal,
require us all to just give in,
each breakthrough a dazzling ideal?
Who thought it a brilliant idea
that all of us gather on-line,
on watch while we browse social media
for someone brand new to malign?

The faraway texts kept on whirling
in brief replies blinking onscreen.
The boy scrolled, each message unfurling —
What else could his girlfriend mean

except that he had to take action?
The time for mere threats was long past.
Reluctance was just one reaction
she knew, with her help, wouldn't last.

His last day was spent at the seashore,
with family who'd brought him along —
The boy, with his golden retriever,
went walking. *Suppose it goes wrong?*
But texts kept on flooding his cellphone
with messages sent and received,
demolishing all hesitation —
He read, and replied, and believed —

You told me you're all set to do it
So what — are you backing out now?
Your family will miss you but screw it
From searching the web I know how
Don't worry — it's totally painless
I'll send someone if you're afraid
You just need your truck and enough gas
to keep the commitment you made

Six days before search parties found her,
a note left behind in her car,
the woman harassed saw, around her,
red oak and birch trees, winter-bare,
the rush of the waterfall calming —
No scorn to diminish its sound,
the branch that she chose reassuring,
and just far enough from the ground.

You'd think the tormenters who drove her
to take her own life would recede
back into the shadows to savor
their work, her disgrace, and her deed.
Instead, when a woman defends her,
they gang up and flame her, renewed,
repeating the same vicious slander,
while racist rants, strangely, intrude.

When will we learn human nature
is worse than we want to admit?
Whose words will crush somebody's future?
What crimes does a stranger commit?
The Web joins, from faraway places
like-minded souls gladly won
to causes so vile and ruthless,
they burn like a cross on the lawn.

A girl's lawyer claims, "There's no case here —
Words aren't a crime," he maintains.
That woman distraught — who erased her?
Each post, undeleted, remains.
The boy's truck was found, engine running,
too late for him. That was the plan —
He got out at one point, still breathing.
The girl texted, *Fucking get in*.

It's hard not to think of the cruelties
we've witnessed or said face to face;
the age-old half-secret societies
that meet in some undisclosed place;
but why does the gift of a keyboard,
cell keypad, or downloaded app

compel the disclosures that, once shared,
entangle us all in their trap?

Whose fury withheld sets the fire?
Whose fury revealed fans the flame?
What sort of hate starts with desire
and ends with a dead woman's name?
Which hatred wakes other resentments
that burn with a core of pure rage,
till all the world cries out for vengeance?
Lord, let me log out of this page.

Cell Phones Lifted in the Public Square

What sign of progress is it
when videos gone viral
capture every shooting
we're helpless to prevent?

Our only choice: to watch,
refuting every frame,
or look at what we see,
bearing collective witness.

Car keys, a toy, a wallet —
some everyday possession
looks just like a gun . . .
Who wouldn't freeze, shoot first?

— Yes, all can be explained
away, ingeniously,
each prop or passerby
vital to the moment.

Who's lost, who's culpable?
The audio fades or fails —
The action's blurred, unsteady,
the watchful eye relentless

&, right on cue, it happens:
a firearm's discharged —
though we close our eyes,
though the view is shaky.

There'll be protests, altercations,
alerts & interviews —
Am I Next? scrawled in chalk
beside a body's outline

& flashing on phones & screens,
footage that never ends . . .
Who calls for an indictment?
Who's listening? Who mourns?

Soon, when twilight vigils
fill the public square,
challenging a narrative
that casts blame on the dead,

the crowd will raise its cell phones,
so many they'll look like stars
viewed from far away —
the distance of history.

Held high, what will they offer?
The light of evidence,
the need for a just verdict,
the promise of contrition,

but the dead keep adding up
& the shootings will go on,
just as they always did,
obscure & unrecorded.

Surveillant of lawful murder,
indifferent to truth, unmoved,
essential & ineffective,
you shine light but change nothing . . .

What must change in *us*
who bear collective witness
to all this grief & guilt
inexorable as ever?

On Trial for an Imaginary Murder

The accusation, strangely, is the proof.
The judge, secure on high, looks unforgiving.
No one takes an oath on your behalf,
sworn to the truth. You feel like an engraving,

powerless to move . . . Who was the victim?
No one says. You're told the prosecution
will defend you, too, since it saves time.
No jury files in for his presentation

of the facts, since no one disagrees.
Will someone raise his voice so you can hear
the case against you? Or the verdict? Freeze
that fraught split second filling you with fear

before you're called? The fan spins overhead —
All eyes are rapt. A bailiff locks the door
and glares. He knows exactly what you did,
and, yes, the evidence will soon assure

your swift conviction in the first degree . . .
But who is that behind you, looking on?
— The murder victim, waiting patiently,
alive and smiling, satisfied she's won.

London Crowds and Tory Crimes

Margaret Thatcher and Tory Minister for the Arts
Norman St. John-Stevas discuss London Calling *ca. 1980*

"And one more thing," she offered, power suit
pristine and sky-blue as she stood and locked
me in her gaze: "This Clash — they're not the Beatles
by a long shot, are they?" "No," I smiled,
"No danger of *that*," I said despite a twinge —
Who knew how far they'd go with brutal youths
stuck on the dole, their prospects fading fast?
She sniffed, a finger on her string of pearls.
"I'm glad — we don't need yet another pop group
calling for revolution from the safety
of the country homes their fortunes bought."
I smiled; she'd every reason to be pleased.
We held the reins at last, the nation ours,
Labour in disarray, backbenchers whipped
into submission, strikers soon to fall,
and all at Number Ten under control.
Control — it's what dear Maggie brought us all.
While would-be rebels wrecked their own guitars
in praise of guns and union hooligans,
cool Tory heads prevailed — and none was cooler
than her own held high beneath dyed hair.
The PM touched a folder on her desk,
fanned out a page or two and looked at me.

"You're not just leader of the House of Commons
Norman, you're Arts Minister as well.
Their songs are calls for riot in the streets —
Can't we arrest them for the public good?"
I wanted to, of course: the wave of "punks"
had mocked authority quite long enough,
I'd learned beyond a doubt when some MP
or his assistant introduced the Clash
via cassette to one of my receptions,
Maurice Chevalier's exquisite duet
from *Gigi* with Hermione Gingold
exchanged for squalls and caterwauls and din.
(They'd thought their prank quite funny till they found
themselves escorted swiftly out the door.)
"Prime Minister, our lads in MI5
pay close attention to the BBC
and hear a good deal unofficially,"
I said, "but, as you know, they take their time.
As for the other options, there are drawbacks.
A drugs arrest is free publicity,
and scandal likelier to win them fans
than bring disgrace." The PM nodded, paused,
as if prepared to wait, and yet, not so —
"Tina" (for There Is No Alternative,
those words she lived by), regal in her bearing,
pressed and spotless, faced me, hesitant,
as she so rarely let herself be seen.
"Prime Minister, is something troubling you?"

"It's 'London Calling,'" she said, "Not the record
but the phrase that every Briton knows
through Wartime broadcasts on the BBC —
Words that told every nation occupied
our help would come, and they were not forgotten.
I heard those words the first time in our flat
above the grocer's that my father owned —
and thought, 'How marvelous it is to live
in England at this dark time in the world,
at history's crossroads when the threat is high
but hope prevails, our very way of life
riding upon the courage of our boys,
our Christian faith, and Mr. Churchill's wits.'
And now, this 'Clash' would twist those very words
into a blow against the Ship of State —
Have they no sense of history, or shame?"
We dropped the subject. Other matters called,
more pressing than the songs of curbside buskers
steeped in Karl Marx, condemned to fade,
their followers drawn from the denizens
of seedy clubs or Hackney council homes
— not our constituency anyway.

I headed home from Number Ten, content
to watch the crowds shift with the London streets
that held our nation's future, and its pain,
the lost, the jobless hordes . . . . I watched the signs
slide over glass along my driver's route,
bright lights and billboards past the roundabout,
our leader's perfume fading . . . Content, I said,
but for the slightest tug, the quiet doubt
that *London Calling* was indeed a call

to those forgotten — not beyond our borders
but here, redundant workers on the dole,
misguided truants hungry for some message
buried in noise, crude beats, bad poetry —
A scream for change the world would not deliver

unless we willed it. And we never would.

Predictions for the President-Elect

January, 2017

It's not in hope or praise I write these words
uneasy in their forecast. Born to privilege,
angry still to think his triumphs less
because of it, our President-Elect
prepares for power. The deals he made or trashed,
the towers he built, emblazoned with his trademark,
all that gold plate, gleaming — none of these
quite compensates for all the slights he's known,
but now? The future is an unmarked page.
Unbowed and scowling even when he smiles,
he's risen higher than he dared to dream
or we could stop. What's next? The world wonders,
shocked awake, while he makes up his mind.
But, Reader, you know more. Words trapped in time —
That's all a poem is. Who can really tell
if, years from now, discovering these lines
in some forgotten corner of the Web,
you'll see them as I do, or differently?
A moment of transition comes and goes,
a pilot light that flashes into flame,
and as I write, time bears us toward events
soon to confront us all — old news to you,
because you're there already, looking back.
Yes, time is good: its course enlightens us.
humbled, we reconsider and reflect —
But is it time to mourn, or wish him well,
this CEO whose tweets and coded speech
diminish rivals and divide us all?

No citizen or legal immigrant,
no child or migrant forced to live in shadows
wants to see a President disgraced,
perhaps not even one whose reckless claims
pervade the news, immune to evidence.
Perhaps he'll finally reverse himself,
submit his wealth to public scrutiny,
denounce for-profit universities,
and steady his restless eye, restrain the conduct
some dismiss as hearsay, nothing proved —
the idle talk of pageant dressing rooms.
Does all his bluster serve as a diversion
from his bold, strategic turn of mind,
our nation's good his first priority?
Will prescience tell us more than precedent?
. . . Reader, my headlines are your history,
all questions posed and answered, doubts resolved.
If you could speak through time, what would you say?
That, years from now, the President-Elect
will be revered, our borderlands secured,
all foreign hacking proved benevolent,
and everyone so prosperous they cheer
or so dead broke, or dead, that they don't matter?
Or will you guard some battered arsenal
against your neighbors, weapon close at hand,
kept warm before a bonfire of old books
remaindered from the past I live in now?
Extreme scenarios! . . . . But if I could
venture a guess quite likely to prove wrong
a few years, not a lifetime, down the road,
we'll find the nation poorer, a little meaner,
the earth's resources mined without regret,

whatever the cost, while factories close down,
more children bearing children of their own,
a corporate compass guiding us abroad,
at home more protests, rural poverty,
and one more life-sized portrait of the man
who looked down from his heights above the skyline
to embrace his destiny, and ours,
removed to storage from a White House wall.

The CEO's Annual Report

Welcome! and greetings from the cutting edge.
This past year we've made strides and great leaps forward,
finalized commitments, forged a bridge
between our old friends and our adversaries —
(wisely, for who knows which is which these days?) —
and having defined new goals worth striving toward,
we've tossed out all the old ones, tattered selves
cast off, vaguely distasteful with the whiff
of yesterday's now not-so-Great Ideas.
And yet, there's much to do. The world revolves,
upon an axis fit for re-invention
every so many years. Do not be stiff,
unyielding, or too slow when Change sweeps in
to clean the last few cluttered areas.

IV.

If 'future' means foreseeing change, there must have been a time — the species' major time — when there wouldn't have been a future; when time was replica, not revolution; when anything that *could* ever happen, *had* happened; and when birth then aging then death took place inside the greater present tense . . . .

Though once the future exists at all, no matter how distant and nebular, it doesn't lie in wait — it flings itself headlong against the grain of time to meet us.

— Albert Goldbarth, "The Future"
in *Great Topics of the World*

Can anyone foretell his future conduct?
    If you were a lion, what kind would you be?
        — Martial, Epigram 12.92, Susan McLean, translator

In Memory of Daniel Hoffman

How even a single image wrests
From oblivion its maker's name.
　　　　— Daniel Hoffman, "Literature"

Daniel, I didn't know you very well,
but you were kind to me because of Poe,
our shared allegiance. Close to ninety, frail,
diminutive and dashing, on the go
and fearless on your own, you drove a car
yacht-sized and ancient. As your passenger,

confined as in some coffin out of Poe,
my wife along, charmed by your erudition,
I watched you drive Ceredo Avenue
the wrong way to the Bearden exhibition,
chatting pleasantly. There, we admired
his *Odyssey* collages — bright, inspired —

the conference crowd surrounding us, your frail
frame in khaki suit against the bench,
your wild gray hair askew . . . Though you were ill,
six years a widower, time did not quench
your dedication to the memory
of early days you spent in New York City,

ex-Air Corps at Columbia, on the go
beside Elizabeth, dear editor
and poet you met by chance, with whom you'd know
shared happiness for decades . . . . In the year
after you'd chauffeured us, I'd hear from you
sometimes, an e-mail: playful — kindly, too —

you spoke your mind as you did in that car,
willing to praise the poems in my new book —
"Far better than the efforts of some scholar,
tenure-bound, who takes one final look
at how to rescue from his dissertation
authors of rightly minor reputation."

I had to smile . . . . Now you're the passenger
who's passed from one realm, with the poems he made,
into another, gracious, ready for
what fame or fate awaits a kindly shade.
Your business card read "Poet Laureate"
— Daniel, your kindness made you more than that.

Ex Libris Lux

Beyond the timeless sycamore, Great Tree
whose bark broke off in curved sheets every season,
Thompson Library looked like a cathedral
brimming with sacred texts. What were its secrets,
shelved and Dewey-tagged? We'd flip through typed
cards, jotting notes (post-its didn't exist),
a thousand drawers inspiring hope or panic
on our quest across the alphabet.

From my dorm room I could see the tower —
carved pinnacles and lancets — past the turrets
of a grand façade that kept its counsel
even when snow-drifts nullified the lawn,
even when spring took hold.
                How strange our passage
must have looked: women in peasant dresses,
hippie chic, or punk plumes spiked to shock;
prep schoolers privileged; Frisbees caught in flight
by guys whose T-shirts told us, *Keep On Truckin'*.
Each year, the spring semester winding down,
dorms blasted music — Dylan, Patti Smith —
while, dazzled, we rode westward with John Donne
or found ourselves marooned with Caliban.
What other music did we hear back then?

— A steady clacking, birdsong, sudden fury,
bell and carriage release, a zip, more clacking,
the Talking Heads' alarmed "Once in a Lifetime"
— spring's white noise, the silence of more thinking.

How strange this edifice from 1905 —
tapestry-hung, high-ceilinged, vigilant,
Great Window in its nave, stained glass aflame —
stood unchanged through it all: the hostage crisis,
gas lines, Skylab's plunge . . . Sometimes we'd see
alumnae from between the World Wars,
pre-coed days: one frail, in sky-blue dress,
another vital, sharp-eyed, standing straight
in old age, gowned and pearled, her own youth's scandals
less than ours — quaint, even, we were sure —
strolling pine-guarded grounds, our own paved walks.

Would we be frail or vital in the future
when, our fashions altered, we'd return
to gawk, surprised by time, technology,
and streaming data nobody can hold?
We were the anachronisms, after all,
not forebears dressed like Bishop or Millay.
Days counting down — fortunate, pastoral —
we lived as if this world belonged to us
and would not change. It would. But less than we.

Time is, thou hast, employ the portion small,
the library clock, ornately carved, advised,
the words inscribed around its numerals,
both heeded and ignored . . .
                              Hungover, hungry,
in love or in a rush, the week near gone,
we'd scatter to the stacks, resolved once more
to reinvent ourselves, each book we found
a new voice taking hold . . .

                    Or else we'd pull
brass handles gently, smell the near-blonde wood,
breathe in the must of yellowed cards or pages —
books, bound volumes, all that history,

assured, deep down, that they'd outlast us all.

Sonnets for Elizabeth Bishop

1. Elegy for Lota

I lived with you, the rainy season over —
ten years' bliss from which I will recover
never — in your house, our "private cloud"
accessible along a mountain road
to cat and toucan, servants, toast and tea.
Men poured cement by your authority;
I wrote, determined to perfect a world
in language where, unthreatened, it might last . . . .
We lit the lamps at dusk; days faded fast.
Quaint iron stove, the vistas I beheld —
they *looked* the same, but what did I expect
in ten years' time, beloved architect?
Love lasts, but *we* don't. When your house was done,
you broke beneath new labors. I was gone.

2. A Toucan in Samambaia

In Samambaia, Sam the toucan thrived,
flea-bitten, azure-eyed, banana-fed,
content with mountain-view when he arrived,
and, poor bird, when he left. Anything red,
bright-edged, or shiny, helped him pass the day,
encaged but loved. His huge beak was the prop
that brought such humor and humility —
Remember how he'd swallow every grape,

a pinball down the gutter? Once, distracted
from some sudden storm, I felt a shock —
Sam's outside! — *Drowned?* I ran but, unprotected,
he'd survived, immobile, gaudy beak
turned skyward, eyes shut, soaked to his blue skin,
amazed: the same condition I was in.

3. Houseguest of an Architect

One cashew after dinner, just a taste,
transformed my life: hours later, weak, afraid,
I found myself bedridden, eyes shut tight,
but glad that illness offered such good reason
to extend my stay. You spoke, and workmen
stopped their hammering . . . . This sleepless night
in your unfinished house, I raise the shade,
the cliff beside us rain-lashed, owl-blessed,
and listen for the proof I've been delivered
from my solitude — not just the waterfall the rain drowns out, frog-bleat or lizard-
skitter on the floor, but past the lamp-glow,
you, asleep: aristocratic daughter,
muse and lover. Rest, and I will follow.

Night Watch

A meme originating from a photo taken at the Rijksmuseum in Amsterdam

We've seen the meme: museum gallery
with Rembrandt's *Night Watch* looming on the wall,
as Captain Cocq, vandyked and armed, sets out,
backed by his company, while teens en masse
stare at their cells, oblivious, on the bench.
They might be tweeting selfies back and forth,
or texting friends, or wasting time on Buzzfeed,
or re-living highlights from their trip
just moments past . . . But why don't they look up?
The point is, they don't see the masterwork.

We've learned to view the whole world through our screens —
how could we live without them? Every day,
they lead us where they will by cell or laptop,
wireless Wi-Fi linked to smart TVs.
What would Rembrandt think to know his soldiers,
muskets charged, have been reduced to code,
frames photoshopped by wags to feature wisecracks,
carried in bits and bytes around the world?
Someone will soon design an app to tell us.
But is it only kids who wake up, drawn

to sounds and icons mediated and mashed
like tracers drifting by to fill our dreams?
What's troubling me right now is not some students
on their field trip — how different are we
who share the Rembrandt meme in snarky threads

while checking status updates? — but the thought
of how the very act of seeing's changed.
Can we still see the world, look at a painting,
anything, with our minds uncluttered, clear
of chatter despite our quest for one last photo

we'll later trash, or scroll past and forget?
We don't look *up* or look *at* anymore
but only *through* or *past,* all that we "share"
bringing what we deserve: a rain of shards.
Screens make the real world seem more real than real,
igniting at the ringtone of our choice.
They know our habits and indulge our whims,
each dark void booting up to light the world.
We love them like we love to look at fire,
twinkling lights, disasters far away,

but can we love the world as much as Rembrandt
who took in every shadow with his eye
and painted every gleam on the brocade
of Cocq's lieutenant? Or as much as those
same teens, awestruck, who peer into their cells
to study the brushwork as they pinch and zoom?
We brought them up and led them to this brink,
a world we put onscreen, where glyphs and icons
dazzle us all among the junk and wisdom
whirling while the world outside grows dim.

Amerika for Erika

Dear Erika, you know not what you do.
Your name's last consonant is not your nation's,
is it? — rhymes aside, no matter how
clever or cool it looks on Xeroxed signs
stuck to the walls of dining halls or dorms.
Nor should you advertise your smiling self
flag-wrapped for your political campaign:
the office you seek isn't national
or statewide, but as local as it gets,
i.e., class president of sophomores
whose votes you'll buy with pizza and free beer.
I know, I know — you're a millennial,
all selfies, hashtags, texts, and vocal fry,
I'm pre-millennial by many years,
your tweets attract more readers than my words,
and spelling — who cares anyway? And yet,
I wonder: do you know what Yippies are?
You're young, and so were they: you share their interest
in democracy — that's good — and, sure,
they're old guys now, or dead, and you don't know
exactly what they stood for in their time,
but let me tell you this: it's not high praise
to trade that "c" for an ironic "k."
Why does it matter now? Your record's clean.
You don't know Abbie Hoffman from *Abbey Road*,
Chicago Seven's just your dad's old vinyl,
and "k" — well, that "k"'s yours: Erika's "k."
I get it. Still, let's both just think a minute —

Whether you're shaking hands, snapchatting friends,
or tapping kegs for games of beer pong
with likely voters, history flows on,
foam-drenched, and takes us with it, young and old,
our memories almost full like some old laptop,
disc, or cell phone — though YOLO, you know,
and youth cloaked in the Stars and Stripes sells more
than spellchecked speeches do. But one more thought.
Did you know you and Abbie share a kinship
that transcends the "k"? That in a scuffle
with police in 1968
before his HUAC testimony, he, too,
dressed in our flag, a shirt that so enraged
the District's finest that they tore it off,
handcuffed and jailed him? They stripped him naked,
sprayed away the lice he didn't have,
drew blood to spook him, locked him in a cell —
one more disoriented radical
who'd tried to levitate the Pentagon
(no, not successfully), who'd desecrate
the nation's symbol with his hair and sweat,
incite a riot, and, yes, dare use a "k"
to spell his country's name. You do that, too,
minus the notoriety and beatings
(thank God), our collective memory
purged of unpleasantness, Old Glory's rights
intact, inviolate . . . Dear Erika,
we've never met. I wish you many years —
whether you spend them in America,
a daughter of fortune in the future's light,
or in Amerika, that darker place
where smiles are wry or bitter . . . With flag-pin fixed

to your lapel, or flag-patch stitched to jeans
in some location not too disrespectful,
may you find your true constituents,
whoever they are. I hope that they'll be loyal —
compassionate, at least, if you must fail —
and may your words add up to more than slogans,
jokes, or jangling rhymes, whether your rise
is meteoric or a long, slow climb:
I won't see either, finally, but you will.
Victorious or not, your smiling face
ripped from the walls, torn up and thrown away,
may you not fail history, but make it
yours, no matter how it's spelled, someday.

Sabbatical

What you find in the outside world is what's escaped from
your own inner world.
     — Ted Hughes

Jobless last fall, kneeling to scratch
the ruffled fur of fearless tortie Jane,
the local cat who shares a borrowed name,
     I looked above & saw

     what she saw first: a red-tailed hawk —
white chest, his broad wings folded, burnished beak
filed to a point. A young bird, beautiful,
     he stared down through gold leaves.

     Were we at risk? . . . The hawk was silent,
the silly tableau of human greeting cat
just one of many follies that he'd witnessed
     in his time, unmoved —

But now the element of surprise
was lost. He flexed his talons, flew away.
What could I do? I half-smiled, kept on walking
     home, still touched with awe

     but troubled, too. Each house I passed,
restored or worn, looked uninhabited,
its occupants away at school or work,
     the jack-o'-lantern dark

till they returned, leaves loose & whirling
overhead . . . I glanced up at a chimney
half a block away: the bird of prey
                  had landed, claimed a place

but also drawn a crowd: 6 crows
(a "murder," it's called) who dove in close & fled,
circling in swift arcs: graceful, black, discordant,
                  threading the sky in flight,

though he held fast to brick. Brave hawk!
But was his temporary territory,
seized on a whim, worth a prolonged defense
                  now that a gang had formed?

Well, no. And when he'd had enough,
the hawk took off, that sleek black-feathered mob
(a minor inconvenience) in pursuit.
                  So what should I conclude?

That lesser birds will bond in fear
& band together for a planned attack
against a common foe forced into exile?
                  That suspicion makes

an enemy of anyone?
That crow-calls are a language of their own,
& every cry a rumor, true or not,
                  that echoes for generations?

Or that the raptor I admired,
whose very presence marked him predator,
had strayed too far from home, his pale eyes
        proof he'd seen too much

    & had no place? I'd seen a lot,
but if I'd kept my counsel like that hawk,
I'd still be nearing dusk, another day
        of my "sabbatical,"

    I called it then — but, no, that wasn't
right: a real sabbatical would end.
Unlike that red-tailed hawk who soon returned,
        I'm never going back.

Wren

The countdown's under way, your flight's departure
sooner than we'd like, but our routine's
small pleasures shape our days . . . And so, returned
from one last grocery trip, I turn the key

when you glimpse, down the hall, a small winged creature
trapped against bright glass. What led this wren's
dead reckoning astray? Tiny, determined
to escape, he flutters, falls away,

caught in the stairwell window where the future
seals him, stuck in place. Now we're his means
to freedom, maybe, if he's not too stunned.
I curl my palm around him, very gently

lift him from the sill. No blood or fracture
evident, he squirms, uneasy, tense —
like us, when after jobless months I found
work out of state. We don't know if I'll stay

or when I'll leave, the fragile architecture
of our lives in doubt, like all our plans —
We're traveling through unfamiliar land,
and yet, we're lucky, like this wren today,

rescued when he resigned himself to capture —
Frail, rust-brown, he'll have a second chance.
But as we reach the lobby, one split-second
from the door, he makes his getaway,

slips from the grasp he simply can't endure,
scrapes tile, then takes flight through the open entrance —
thankless, free. Must every visit end
sadly, too soon? Our wren crashed helplessly,

unharmed, on unseen glass, a force of nature
furious, compressed . . . If there are omens,
signs it's possible to understand,
we'll watch for them: together, separately.

Ames, Iowa

Station in Disrepair with Lost Frontier

On 364ᵗʰ Road, Seward, Nebraska

We felt misled but weren't: the seedy station's
red-for-stop GAS sign lured us from 80
to its stained no-longer-white oasis

of generic fuel. The other sign
that greeted us — *Sinclair,* with brontosaurus
cast in green — looked down as we drove in,

the station's logo only months ago:
the last brand sold before the franchise failed.
Both ways we looked, the county road seemed endless —

cornfields, scattered trailers, power lines
converging with the sky, our only choice
a pair of gas pumps on a battered island.

I swiped a card, fueled up while you went in,
then followed as the cashier turned and glared,
mute at her post, arrivals scrutinized —

(Well, what was there to do to pass the time,
nothing for sale among the vacant racks,
bare aisles and shelves empty of inventory?

No wonder I wasn't made to feel welcome
in a place of absolute neglect.)
The men's room was — well, what did I expect? —

nor was I too surprised to read the words
wrought by some careful hand amid the gang
graffiti and crude art: *To the cashier lady*

up front: you're very attractive. Just so you know.
Some traveler's joke: she stood guard warily,
a few stray Pepsis huddled in the one

last fridge still powered and lit . . . But what else did
a stranger's barb convey at her expense?
That she, a woman immigrant, alone,

could be insulted with impunity?
Or that, days later, when she found the message,
bent with a brush beside the men's room stall,

it would demean her more if she believed it —
a flash, till she caught on? Or was is that
the old, the odd, the poor deserve our scorn?

Our Mapquest printout folded on your lap
(no GPS), we buckled up to leave,
our fuel's unwitting prehistoric source

presiding overhead and underground,
lost mascot, saurian in silhouette,
who knew more than we did about extinction —

when, across the way, another ruin
we'd driven past the first time beckoned us:
A frontier town, some failed roadside attraction

in collapse, wood structures warped and weathered,
labeled in white paint strangely luminous,
SALOON, A H CORRAL, LIVERY, a wagon

shattered against the prairie, overgrown;
and where the acreage stopped, a plywood sign
(three sheets propped up and joined by rusted wire)

offered its words in vivid capitals,
A DREAM DIED HERE, impossible to miss.
We weren't misled, but chance had brought us here

to learn that time will find an audience
for every urgent message, cursed or cursive,
hurtful and small, or framed in words so huge

we only have to glance in their direction
to confront the size of its despair,
ambition's magnitude, fulfilled or thwarted,

fury drawn to scale . . . . As we'd passed,
I'd slowed down for a better look, but why?
We weren't that sign's intended readers, were we,

but only travelers heading west together
through Nebraska's flatlands . . . Down the ramp
I gunned the engine. "Let's get out of here."

My Birth Father's Mug Shot

I know that look: surprised, a little dazed,
ashamed at being caught, transported here
against your will to face the camera's shutter
for this female officer in blue
(or gray, or khaki) calling out your name
as you recoil, suspended in the flash.
It couldn't have been easy to relive
those teenage joyrides spoiled by an arrest,
the county squad car this time drawing near
along a coastal road in Florida
twelve years ago, though I just found out now.
What crime did you commit? I'd have to pay
to find out what the charge was — probably
a DUI — nothing extravagant —
though, yes, a mug shot's still embarrassing.

It's just as well you don't know that it's here,
this jpeg posted for the world to see,
the beard you've worn since 1969
completely white, your sweatshirt heather-gray.
You look as if you're looking out at me,
except — you're not. It's strange to see you now.

Eighteen or so, I worked for you two summers,
willing to think our bond could be repaired —
if by *repaired* I meant *exist at all*.
The only mother I'd ever known was dying —
The father who'd raised me, Carmine, out of work,

no plumber's job in sight; and so, your wife —
my birth mother—urged you to hire us
— Perhaps, with Betty terminally ill,
the feud between sisters, finally, would end.
The auto radiator chain you'd built
had brought prosperity, a Cadillac
as gold as all that bore your Midas touch . . .
You could afford to be magnanimous.

That summer, as your employee, not your son
(except to those who knew, or guessed, the truth),
I'd seen you kneel, talk gently to the boys
born once our mother had become your wife,
our tangled history tangled even more —
and you were kind to Carmine on the job,
offering to support a plumbing business
on your premises, its bond and fees
requiring thousands far beyond our means.
He'd need a Master's License of his own —
I helped him study. You paid for the test.

What kind of vessel are you sailing now,
near Florida, Key Largo, the Bahamas,
or beyond St. Croix? Long Island men,
it seems, can't sweat the sea air from their blood,
nor all the oil, smoke, and gasoline
sent coursing through their lives; but seeing you
against a blue sky in that final summer
on the only sail we shared one weekend
afternoon, my brothers children still,
our mother riding with you over waves
pristine and steady, I could see the man

you thought you were: a man too smart, too strong
to waste time looking back, your clear gaze trained
ahead beyond the mast toward some horizon
out of reach but always within sight;
a man — a father — who controlled his fate
and that of three sons borne along this journey
as supporting players in the drama
of his triumph, the salt wind whipping wildly
through your hair and jacket, ours as well.

I know that look — surprised, a little dazed —
because I've seen it on my own face, too,
the look I must have worn when Carmine told me
how, a few months after he was widowed,
you could calmly sit behind your desk
and counsel him to sign away our house,
its upkeep more than he could now afford,
its deed fair trade and rightful compensation
for your huge investment, the returns
you'd counted on too slowly trickling in.
He refused, and when I left for school,
you laid him off for good.
                              With Carmine purged,
how could you call to ask if I'd return?
You'd hoped to claim the little we had left.
How strong must we be to remake ourselves —
how focused and how ruthless?
                              By this time,
I doubt you ever think about the way
your fingers, lifting, left their lasting imprint
on the paper underneath your name,
identity confirmed, the past that shaped you,

long erased, abruptly flooding back.
What did you see beyond that frozen instant,
peering from your photo past the flash?

A hundred bucks will take the mug shot down,
proof of arrest expunged. In time, I'll pay
as if to clear my conscience, or your own,
for what we never shared: who knows what wrongs
weigh heavily on you, what costs you bear,
whose words would tip the balance in your favor?
And yet, I'll wait: it's comforting to know
there's somewhere I can look at you sometimes,
the image unmistakably your own
rising with every search that bears your name,
a brief flash seen before it disappears —
your face amazed, remorseful — one last time.

For my birth father Don O —, December 27, 2004
and ca. 1978; and for Carmine

Elegy with a Memory of Starlight

"The painter came, and all the animals which had decorated the walls were being painted over . . . ." It was then that her father pasted up the stars.

What magic did you practice in the dark,
the ceiling stars you loved still shining down
in memory, or in imagination?

The myths you stitched for children cast their spell
on all of us: you swept down from some world
we'd never know in clothes you'd sewn yourself,

your red hair shining when you tossed your head,
or rode your bike cross-campus in the spring.
Your laughter rang out joyfully. You spoke

of Rilke, Blake, and Silko — Bishop, too —
while we sat, awed, or watched you while you listened,
wondering what secrets you'd reveal

when you replied . . . A tiger, burning bright,
pawed at the rug as if in friendly welcome
at the door of Blake's inn while, at home,

you alchemized sports headlines into poems,
or summoned kitchen magic into words
as bright as onion-light, as dark as soil

that tugged the roots of parsnips in their sleep —
The earthy darkness that could never claim you,
we believed, given the light you shared,

the myths you wove, the grace you freely gave.
Tonight, are you among the real stars,
the animals beneath the paint restored

along the walls inside your childhood room?
Readers will keep your night sky burning bright . . .
Your kindly magic drives away the dark.

For Nancy Willard, 1936-2017

The Dark

Each day, we wake to crisis,   *Is*
a new age of unreason,   *reason*
its rage impossible   *possible,*
to counter or ignore.   *or*
A small light, like a star   *are*
behind us, shadowy,   *we*
flares brightly for a moment,   *meant*
grows dim . . . . What should we do?   *to*
The dark provides no template —   *let*
We're caught beyond our power,   *our*
some unknown destination   *nation*
awaiting us . . . In free fall,   *fall?*

burned by the atmosphere,   *Fear*
will we survive? With what   *what*
scant payload, what supplies?   *lies*
What quake or thunderhead   *ahead,*
will follow when we land?   *and*

Hold on, and brace for impact.   *act.*

A Wreath for Doctor Morbius

Forbidden Planet, 1956

I

Dear Morbius, it's time to face the truth.
Marooned on Altair 4 for 19 years,
alone but for your daughter and a robot
stalwart, strong, and shockingly polite,
you're angry at the would-be rescuers
whose mission is to take you back to Earth
and teach your pretty daughter how to kiss.
You're lost in studies of an ancient race
whose minds could make a stray thought tangible . . .
So when, on cue, some force that no one sees
starts tearing wayward crewmen limb from limb,
we guess that you're responsible, somehow.

And then it dawns on us: that force *is* you —
The shadow-self that Freud identified
now independent and invisible —
The side effect of lost technology.
You're just as shocked as your unwelcome guests
to find your dark Unconscious given form —
"A monster from the id!" that leaves its tracks
in sand beside the bodies in its wake.

You save the crew by blowing up the world,
but not before your teenager in love
escapes with those whose meddling fed your rage,
Robbie, his circuits blinking, by her side.

II

Don't blame yourself. You thought the ancient gadget
had increased your brainpower — nothing more.
The glyphs you could decipher didn't say
that vanished race — the Krell — had gone extinct
the same way, murdered by their own dark id,
by violence long suppressed, collective feelings
called up by undying energy
produced by indestructible machines.

Plucked from the scene before you doomed yourself,
what would you say if you could see us now,
time-travelling from your far, forbidden planet
to our savvy, tech-enlightened time?
A time when every cell phone flares, alight —
An era when we, too, project our thoughts
across the globe at will, and the reply
of every mind logged into each device
deceives us into thinking we are wise?

Like the Krell, we've learned to map the stars
and split the atom, masters of the world.
Could we, too, perish in a single night,
even without their mind-expanding tech,
the monsters from our own ids magnified
10 to the power of infinity?
It's possible, you'd say. We have the means.
Uploaded and updated, thread by thread,
we tear each other and ourselves apart...

But we survive, our monsters close at hand,
hiding behind our masks to post the carnage
easy to deny, who stalk and shame
and seek the stars in all that we destroy.

May you live on in memory for the way
you sacrificed yourself with those machines
that hummed eternally and summoned murder
from the starless, unacknowledged void.

Sea Star

In water cobalt-blue a sea star melts,
its five rays torn away to join the silt's
        suspension, sand, and clay,
a spent core all that's left; and when it wilts,
imploding into white pulp, nothing else
        remains — a mystery

whose cause we fear... Some poison in the pulse
of coastal waves, some pathogen in swells
        sun-warmed and placid? Why
would constellations die amid the shells
and octopi, volcanic barnacles
        and dim, aquatic sky

where satellites collide in soundless trails?
The star's a predator. It targets snails,
        vulnerable prey
slow-moving, stationary. Clasped, it pulls
small armored shells apart before it kills
        piecemeal, deliberately:

the stomach through its mouth extends and fills,
withdraws again, digesting. What foretells
        its own fate undersea?
Whole colonies, as if devoured, convulse,
dividing, dying in some fatal impulse,
        nothing we can see

responsible . . . . What's killing auklets, gulls,
egrets, an ark's escort of flailing mammals —
       bruised sea lions who lie
beached on Pacific shores? Is it the krill's
diminishment, or something else that fails
       or breaks down in decay,

       invisible to see? A sea star melts,
its flesh dissolving in a sea where guilt's
       past knowledge, astral body
trapped in place, split from an eye that dwells
where each ray terminates and twilight falls
       or fades uncertainly.

Heirs of Knossos

After "Forbidden Fruit," Andrew Leicester, artist;
terra cotta and metal, 1991.
Molecular Biology Building, Iowa State University

Arms wide, the goddess brandishes two snakes —
Minoans thought: *protectors of the home.*
The Dionysian cults: *fertility.*
Which thread, unfolding slowly, tells us, *Come?*

A stylized sculpture on a pedestal,
she peers out from her helmet, pale, severe,
alert for ways to demonstrate her power.
Her snakes: the DNA strands in each fist —

She's not the first. Knossos produced her sisters,
idols unknown, unearthed. Volcanic quakes
gave way to war, a Roman colony,
but those snake-handling deities endured

bodiced, bare-breasted . . . . Here, their watchful cousin,
cloaked within her hazmat suit of armor,
guards the sky-lit space and atrium,
a goddess for our times: a scientist.

From pure mind, the phylogenetic tree
takes root and spreads. The double helix breaks
into its separate strands, adds to each sum.
We're watching. What new genesis awakes?

Chimeras for the bioethicist —
Diversions that transcend a single genome.
The heir of Knossos was the Minotaur,
lost in the Labyrinth . . .

Is it your wisdom,

Goddess, we should see his face again,
unloved and hungry, waiting for the spark
of distant torches, stars that leave no trace?

The strands you hold will lead him from the dark.

What Words Survive

*23 "ultraconserved" words — cognates across four or more
language families — derive from an ancestral tongue spoken
over 15,000 years ago during the Ice Age.*

What words of ours survive both ice and fire
crackling while predators watch us from afar?
Concealed in our very speech is who we are,

the world we named beneath a glacier.
Mother and Man. At night, we heard a river
flowing and flowed, far from both ice and fire —

The river the old men woke us up to hear,
cold surge they said was deepening every year.
Concealed in our very speech is who we are:

Hunters who broke the earth and spoke a prayer
in praise of the worm. We looked toward the evening star,
seeking a word that fused both ice and fire,

or pulled back our hands from a blaze that leapt too near.
Black ashes and embers spitting, we'd poke and stir —
Concealed in this very speech is who we are:

Gatherers of words and worlds, huddled together,
braiding the bark we stripped into rope and wonder.
Give thanks we survived, you and I, both ice and fire —
Not as flesh, but as words in the very speech we are.

Artificial Age

Mr. Nelson, Mr. Nelson, can you hear my voice? . . .
The medication you were given has put you in a suspended
animation for quite some time — well, in fact, forty-five years —
but where you are now, is in a place that doesn't require time . . .
And we are here to help you.

Would you believe me if I told you Prince
is still alive? His master plan's all there
on *Art Official Age*, in affirmations

hip to hypersleep. Cue the suspense
of lucid dreams, suspended animation's
triumph over time. Finally, a voice —

female, South London-tinged — will break in, gently;
violins, bass lines & soothing beats
will end jam session dreams that lasted years —

& Prince will wake. But when? Their roles reversed,
Lianne will keep him calm: the time he slept
was nearly half a century & now

telepathy's the norm. Will he feel shocked?
Of course not. He recorded this CD
& wrote the songs. He'll gaze out through the lens

(3 lenses, actually: 2 for his eyes,
one for the 3rd Eye wisdom on his brow)
& see we're all connected: distant suns

like stars in orbit gleam on triple shades
& blue sky's everywhere: the view is cosmic.
All are one, Lianne intones & Prince,

whom she calls "Mr. Nelson" in respect
& awe, smiles slightly in the white light's halo
spinning like a silver disc in flight.

I like to think he's listening right now —
that Prince hears everything — all sound & music
1 wave, audible — in hibernation

deep in Paisley Park where, like a child
who learns French while she sleeps, he'll wake, reborn
& fluent. In that Artificial Age,

or Age of Art to which we should aspire,
his sleep is temporary, science fiction
tropes aside, the old divisions gone,

& all are blessed, transformed by love & music.
Yes, Prince is still alive & we'll believe
whoever's there to wake & welcome him.

For The Voyagers

The petroglyphs, the crop circles, the skulls
so disproportioned, disinterred remains
of ancient graves, star-maps on cavern walls,
the myths of gods and demigods; the shards
of iron magnetized, squashed batteries
that carbon-dating proves are Neolithic,
maybe; UFOs that cross by night
and vanish; Area 51; the lies,
the cover-ups, the wild-eyed accusations,
lost time, recovered memories, exams
on steel tables, pain; abduction tours
across the cosmos…All these, in the end,
prove nothing. Still, somewhere, in deepest space,
Voyagers 1 and 2 will meet our makers
or greet those we've made (in our own image,
mostly, faces strange, wide-eyed, benign,
so we believe), their scanned telemetry
fading with time and distance, though each probe
bears, bolted to its side, a golden record
of our world, sleeved in a gilded shield:
whale-song and Bach, wind-blasts, the surf's retreat,
bird-calls and greetings in Sumerian
and other languages extinct or spoken,
images from around the globe, rain forests,
ocean floors . . . And, yes, the diagrams
intended to make playback child's play
shine from each album cover that protects
its trove from space-dust, interstellar storms;

the symbols of our Earth, engraved with care,
persist, gold-tinted: disc and stylus, sound
and video wave, binary code, and more:
our Sun's location, star-map of our own,
from Us to Them, an open invitation
that declares, Come visit in the future
when, eons away, we'll be long gone
but (knock wood) our descendants will be waiting
still, with open arms, our message etched
in what, to me, looks quite suspiciously
like Neolithic drawings on cave-walls,
mysterious symbols of a long-lost world,
abstract designs, crop circles, petroglyphs —
our cuneiform of longing, and our song.

Notes

Rare Book and Reader: For more information, see the on-line Vassar Encyclopedia, "Interviews and Reflections" section: "Ron Patkus on Vassar College Special Collections."

The Underground Tour: "As you roam the subterranean passages that once were the main roadways and first-floor storefronts of old downtown Seattle, our guides regale you with the stories our pioneers didn't want you to hear." (Ad copy for the Underground Tour).

High Strangeness: J. Allen Hynek's words appear in *UFO's: A Scientific Debate*, edited by Carl Sagan and Thornton Page (Norton, 1974). See also the widely shared diagram "commonly reported UFO types."

A Word the Romans Used: The epigraph is from Dana Gioia's essay "Poetry as Enchantment" which first appeared in *The Dark Horse* [20th Anniversary Issue] 34: 2015.

My Millay: See the chapter "Renascence" in Daniel Mark Epstein's *What Lips My Lips Have Kissed: the Loves and Love Poems of Edna St. Vincent Millay* (Holt, 2002).

To Genesis and Back: The epigraph source is "Genesis I," Pliney Earle Goddard, translator (1909), after Cahto narrator Bill Ray and published in editor Jerome Rothenberg's *Technicians of the Sacred* (University of California Press, 1985). In *The Great Animal Orchestra*, musician/author Bernie Krause warns, "Little by little the vast orchestra of life, the chorus of the natural world, is in the process of being quietened" (Back Bay Books, 2013).

Musicology: "In 2004, Prince donated $30,000 to Chanhassen Elementary School. To honor Prince's love of music, a portion of the funds [was] used to buy a Yamaha electric piano" (*Chanhassen Villager*, 28 April 2016).

Belated Aubade: Zach Condon's "A Sunday Smile" appears on Beirut's chanson-inspired *The Flying Club Cup* (4AD, 2007).

Live from the Dakota: The Manhattan building where John Lennon lived and outside of which he was shot.

Full Circle: The italicized lyric is from "Little Green," on Joni Mitchell's *Blue* (Reprise, 1971); the epigraph is from "The Circle Game" which closes *Ladies of the Canyon* (Reprise, 1970).

The Ghosts of Thunder Road: For the epigraph, see "Thunder Road," the opening track of *Born to Run* (Columbia, 1975). A ghost observes the narrator of Bruce Springsteen's song. "Tillie" is Asbury Park's familiar archaic smiling face.

Tinker to Evers to Chance: Scott Miller continued to record and release outstanding music through the 1990s before The Loud Family's swan song, *Attractive Nuisance* (Alias, 2000), which features a cover photo of the empty Burnt Norton pool.

Season of Elliott: When he died at thirty-four, Steven Paul ("Elliott") Smith was thought by many to be the finest rock songwriter of his generation. He performed "Miss Misery" at the March 1998 Oscars ceremony. He didn't win.

Groovy Decay: Mark Deming at the *Allmusic* website: "Robyn Hitchcock has never made a secret of the fact that he has little use for his second solo album, 1982's *Groovy Decay*." The Venus 3 are Peter Buck (of R.E.M.), Scott McCaughey (of Young Fresh Fellows and The Minus 5), and Bill Rieflin (of many bands).

The Bryn Mawr graduate program in English is no more, as confirmed by "College To Trim Programs Bryn Mawr Plan: Stave Off Shortfall" [sic], *Philadelphia Enquirer*, May 3, 1987, archived at *Philly.com*.

Patti in Orbit: "Quaalude orbit beyond the solar asteroid belt" is from then-*Miscellany News* reporter David Duncan's review of Patti Smith's Vassar College Chapel concert, published April 14, 1979, a helpful jog to my own memory.

Star Child: For the epigraph, see "Mothership Connection (Star Child)" on Parliament's *Mothership Connection* (Casablanca, 1975). According to Clinton in *Brothas Be, Yo Like George, Ain't That Funkin' Kinda Hard on You?: A Memoir* (Atria, 2014), "Star Child . . . was an alien who brought funk to Earth. I folded in the *Chariots of the Gods* mythology, sprinkled some contemporary science fiction on the top, and stirred it all together."

Rescuing the Voices: Nine-year-old soloist Sheila Behman sings Don Henley and Glenn Frey's "Desperado"; Hans Louis Fenger is conductor/arranger and guitarist/pianist for the Langley Schools recordings of 1976-77. The epigraph is from Irwin Chusid's liner notes to the CD *Innocence and Despair: The Langley School Music Project* (Bar/None, 2001).

Animal College: "Something is amiss when whole classes of universities have more administrators than faculty. Benjamin Ginsburg's *The Fall of the Faculty* (Oxford University Press, 2011) is an evidence-based broadside that charts the rise of what he calls 'deanlets,' 'deanlings,' and an 'administrative blight' within higher education" (Michael J. Cripps, "The Faculty Administrator." *Inside Higher Ed*, 12 May 2014). MOOC : Massive Open Online Course.

As to why the pigs and dogs of Orwell's *Animal Farm* grow rich without noticeable improvement in other animals' lives: "Perhaps this was partly because there were so many pigs and so many dogs . . . . Much of [their] work was of a kind that the other animals were too ignorant to understand" — or so the pigs and dogs maintain.

Dream Songs for the Governor of Michigan: "For the past two years, the 100,000 people of Flint, Michigan, have been forced to use a poisoned public water system, causing disabling and likely even fatal health effects." (Sen. Don Reagle, "The Flint Water Crisis," *Huffington Post*, 3 February 2016).

London Crowds and Tory Crimes: I have no evidence that Margaret Thatcher ever discussed the Clash with Arts Minister Norman St. John-Stevas, although his musical tastes may be confirmed on-line at *BBC – Desert Island Discs* (June 7, 1975 broadcast).

In Memory of Daniel Hoffman: The on-line journal *Per Contra* featured a Festschrift in celebration of Daniel Hoffman's 90th birthday in issue 27, Spring 2013. He died just a few days short of that milestone.

Ex Libris Lux: See "Campus Curio," by Bernice Lippitt Thomas, in *Vassar: The Alumnae/i Quarterly*, Fall 2004.

Elegy for Lota: "In Lota, [Bishop] had found the most profound love of her life . . . . When Lota invited Elizabeth to live with her in Samambaia, and offered to construct a studio for her behind the new house, she said, 'It just meant everything to me.'" Barbara Page, *Elizabeth Bishop: A Growing Legacy* (Vassar College Libraries, 2004).

A Toucan in Samambaia: "I wish you had known the toucan, Sammy, I had for years in Brazil, though. They don't talk, but are really the funniest birds in the world." (Elizabeth Bishop in a letter to Louise Crane, March 10, 1969.)

Houseguest of an Architect: "Leaving Santos, Bishop stopped in Rio de Janiero to visit acquaintances…including the lively, cosmopolitan, well-connected Lota de Macedo Soares . . . . By fortuitous misfortune, Bishop was stricken with a severe allergic reaction to the fruit of the cashew nut that delayed her departure — a delay that stretched into some seventeen years' residence in Brazil." Barbara Page, *Elizabeth Bishop: A Growing Legacy* (Vassar College Libraries, 2004).

Amerika for Erika: See Nadine Bloch's article "The day they levitated the

Pentagon" at *Waging Non-Violence: People-Powered News and Analysis* (October 21, 2012) and "The Trial of Abbie Hoffman's Shirt" by Paul Krassner, at *The Huffington Post* (May 25, 2011).

Sabbatical: Epigraph source: Ted Hughes interview quoted by Keith Sagar in "Fourfold vision in Hughes," *The Achievement of Ted Hughes*, Manchester University Press, 1983.

Elegy with a Memory of Starlight: The epigraph is from "Portrait of Newberry Medalist Nancy Willard," *The Horn Book*, August 17, 1982.

Sea Star: "The living sea has now become a killer. And all it took was a little extra added heat to lock west coast waters into an expanding zone of warm water and low oxygen marine mortality." See Robert Fanney, "Starving Sea Pups and Liquefied Starfish: How We've Turned the Eastern Pacific into a Death Trap for Marine Species," February 27, 2015.

Heirs of Knossos: From the plaque beside the sculpture: "Many of the goddess figures that have been excavated hold snakes in their outstretched arms . . . Instead of holding snakes in each hand, however, Leicester's sculpture holds strands of DNA that she has just split apart. In a sense, she is giving birth, since DNA holds the key of life and reproduces by splitting. This goddess is wearing a metallic contamination suit similar to those used in some scientific experiments. Her brain is exposed through the top of the helmet and from these roots the phylogenetic tree extends its branches."

What Words Survive: From "The lifespan of 23 words," David L. Ulin, *Los Angeles Times*, May 8, 2013: "For the record, here is the list: *thou, I, not, that, we, to give, who, this, what, man/male, ye, old, mother, to hear, hand, fire, to pull, black, to flow, bark, ashes, to spit, worm* . . . . Some words seem obvious and elemental: *fire, hand, give, mother, man*. Others are more surprising on the surface, but perhaps not so much when you consider them a bit . . . ."

Artificial Age: Lianne La Havas provides the voice-over in Prince's "Clouds," *Art Official Age* (NPG/Warners, 2014).

For the Voyagers: The Voyager space probes launched from Cape Canaveral aboard Titan-Centaur rockets on August 20 and September 5, 1977. See also Carl Sagan's *Murmurs of Earth: The Voyager Interstellar Record* (Ballantine, 1978). Much fascinating hokum — or provocative theorizing, depending on your viewpoint — may be found in Erich von Däniken's *Chariots of the Gods: Unsolved Mysteries of the Past* (Putnam, 1968).

The Author

Ned Balbo is the author of *The Trials of Edgar Poe and Other Poems* (awarded the Poets' Prize and the Donald Justice Prize), *Lives of the Sleepers* (Ernest Sandeen Prize and *ForeWord* Book of the Year Gold Medal), *Galileo's Banquet* (Towson University Prize co-winner), and *Upcycling Paumanok*. The recipient of a National Endowment for the Arts translation fellowship, three Maryland Arts Council grants, the Robert Frost Foundation Poetry Award, and the John Guyon Literary Nonfiction Prize, he has held fellowships or residencies at the Sewanee Writers' Conference, the Vermont Studio Center, and the Virginia Center for the Creative Arts.

Balbo's poetry, prose, and translations appear in print or online at *Able Muse*, *Birmingham Poetry Review*, *The Common*, *The Dark Horse*, *The Hopkins Review*, *Iowa Review*, *Literary Matters*, *Measure*, *New Criterion*, *Poetry Daily*, *Scoundrel Time*, *Verse Daily*, and many more. Anthology appearances include work in the Everyman's Library volumes *Villanelles* and *Monster Verse: Poems Human and Inhuman* (Knopf), *Air Fare: Stories, Poems, and Essays on Flight* (Sarabande), *Veils, Halos, Shackles: International Poetry on the Oppression and Empowerment of Women* (Kasva), and *Drawn to Marvel: poems from the comic books* (Minor Arcana).

Balbo holds degrees from Vassar College, the Writing Seminars at Johns Hopkins, and the Iowa Writers' Workshop. He is married to poet-essayist Jane Satterfield and was recently a visiting faculty member in the MFA program in Creative Writing and Environment at Iowa State University.

- Final line, p.24
- Half-rhyme, ends w/ full —25
- Not the headiness of
  modn ptry that
  damaged its status/value
  (if such existed), but
  its <u>airheadiness</u>.
- Or poetry centered on
  the "heart" or experience
  is not exempt from
  the demands of head

- Auden on how he approaches poets
  - Bubbo the man
- Proust & light stuff — what is the content?
- Careful: too many poets hide behind the
  - security of choosing the right edicts
  - Concrete vs ideas (abstract) · Verse/not · Contemp
    light/serious · Philo/Nerts · Literate/not

- Ptry is a mansion w/ many rooms
- This one still has the Beatles poster up...
- Italicization -93
- Breaking voice in final line -98
- maintains ~~pod~~ iambic meter
- p.100 -uncertain antecedent
- ?'s -p.100 -as in prose, abuse of rhtrcl ?'s suggests. "This wld be an intrstg essay/argmnt/poem" (Fiction writers cannot do this)

- Shorter meters suit him better
- "That's it?"
- ☆ Calliope ⚥ The Magpies -Poetry